ISBN 978-1-332-96770-4
PIBN 10444363

1 MONTH OF
FREE
READING

at

www.ForgottenBooks.com

By purchasing this book you are eligible for one month membership to ForgottenBooks.com, giving you unlimited access to our entire collection of over 700,000 titles via our web site and mobile apps.

To claim your free month visit:

www.forgottenbooks.com/free444363

English
Français
Deutsche
Italiano
Español
Português

www.forgottenbooks.com

Mythology Photography **Fiction**
Fishing Christianity **Art** Cooking
Essays Buddhism Freemasonry
Medicine **Biology** Music **Ancient
Egypt** Evolution Carpentry Physics
Dance Geology **Mathematics** Fitness
Shakespeare **Folklore** Yoga Marketing
Confidence Immortality Biographies
Poetry **Psychology** Witchcraft
Electronics Chemistry History **Law**
Accounting **Philosophy** Anthropology
Alchemy Drama Quantum Mechanics
Atheism Sexual Health **Ancient History**
Entrepreneurship Languages Sport
Paleontology Needlework Islam
Metaphysics Investment Archaeology
Parenting Statistics Criminology
Motivational

DREN'S LONGFELLOW
Illustrated

HTON MIFFLIN COMPANY

BOSTON & NEW YORK

1908

PUBLISHERS' NOTE

LONGFELLOW has been fitly called the children's poet. Many of his poems have from their first appearance been favorites with youthful readers, and they have been widely used in the schools, but heretofore there has been no comprehensive collection of the poems best adapted for children's reading. It is believed, therefore, that this book will find a ready welcome at the hands of young people and their parents.

The poems here printed have been divided into groups which follow, in a general way, the arrangement in the Cambridge Edition of Longfellow's Poems. With three exceptions, each poem is reprinted in its entirety. In the case of Evangeline, The Song of Hiawatha, and The Courtship of Miles Standish it has been necessary to make a selection of one or two complete divisions from each.

Boston, 1908.

CONTENTS

CONTENTS

CONTENTS

ix

ILLUSTRATIONS

VOICES
OF
THE NIGHT

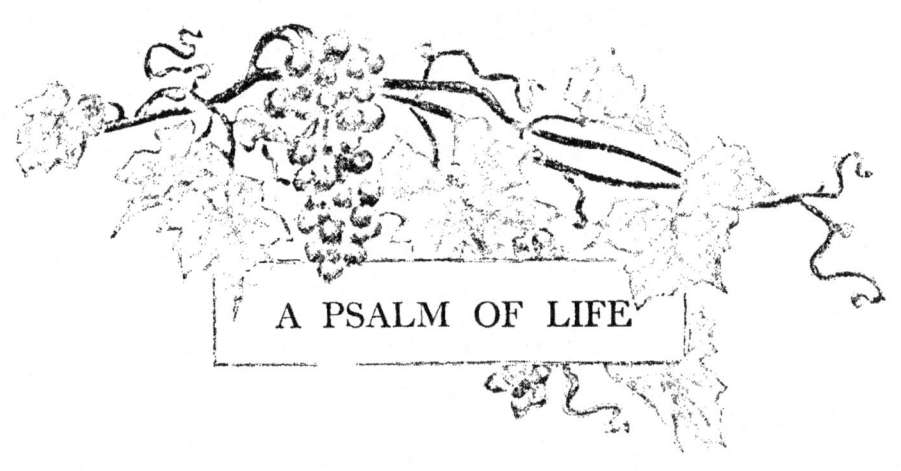

A PSALM OF LIFE

TELL me not, in mournful numbers,
　　Life is but an empty dream ! —
For the soul is dead that slumbers,
　　And things are not what they seem.

Life is real ! Life is earnest !
　　And the grave is not its goal ;
Dust thou art, to dust returnest,
　　Was not spoken of the soul.

Not enjoyment, and not sorrow,
　　Is our destined end or way ;
But to act, that each to-morrow
　　Find us farther than to-day.

Art is long, and Time is fleeting,
　　And our hearts, though stout and brave,
Still, like muffled drums, are beating
　　Funeral marches to the grave.

3

A PSALM OF LIFE

In the world's broad field of battle
    In the bivouac of Life,
Be not like dumb, driven cattle!
    Be a hero in the strife!

Trust no Future, howe'er pleasant!
    Let the dead Past bury its dead!
Act, — act in the living Present!
    Heart within, and God o'erhead!

Lives of great men all remind us
    We can make our lives sublime,
And, departing, leave behind us
    Footprints on the sands of time;

Footprints, that perhaps another,
    Sailing o'er life's solemn main,
A forlorn and shipwrecked brother,
    Seeing, shall take heart again.

Let us, then, be up and doing,
    With a heart for any fate;
Still achieving, still pursuing,
    Learn to labor and to wait.

THE LIGHT OF STARS

THE night is come, but not too soon;
   And sinking silently,
All silently, the little moon
   Drops down behind the sky.

There is no light in earth or heaven
   But the cold light of stars;
And the first watch of night is given
   To the red planet Mars.

Is it the tender star of love?
   The star of love and dreams?
Oh no! from that blue tent above
   A hero's armor gleams.

And earnest thoughts within me rise,
   When I behold afar,
Suspended in the evening skies,
   The shield of that red star.

O star of strength! I see thee stand
   And smile upon my pain;
Thou beckonest with thy mailèd hand,
   And I am strong again.

He rises in my breast,
Serene, and resolute, and still,
    And calm, and self-possessed.

And thou, too, whosoe'er thou art,
    That readest this brief psalm,
As one by one thy hopes depart,
    Be resolute and calm.

Oh, fear not in a world like this,
    And thou shalt know erelong,
Know how sublime a thing it is
    To suffer and be strong.

FLOWERS

Spake full well, in language quaint and olden,
  One who dwelleth by the castled Rhine,
When he called the flowers, so blue and golden,
  Stars, that in earth's firmament do shine.

Stars they are, wherein we read our history,
  As astrologers and seers of eld;
Yet not wrapped about with awful mystery,
  Like the burning stars, which they beheld.

Wondrous truths, and manifold as wondrous,
  God hath written in those stars above;
But not less in the bright flowerets under us
  Stands the revelation of his love.

Bright and glorious is that revelation,
  Written all over this great world of ours;
Making evident our own creation,
  In these stars of earth, these golden flowers.

And the Poet, faithful and far-seeing,
  Sees, alike in stars and flowers, a part
Of the self-same, universal being,
  Which is throbbing in his brain and heart.

These in flowers and men are more than seeming,
    Workings are they of the self-same powers,
Which the Poet, in no idle dreaming,
    Seeth in himself and in the flowers.

Everywhere about us are they glowing,
    Some like stars, to tell us Spring is born;
Others, their blue eyes with tears o'erflowing,
    Stand like Ruth amid the golden corn;

Not alone in Spring's armorial bearing,
    And in Summer's green-emblazoned field,
But in arms of brave old Autumn's wearing,
    In the centre of his brazen shield;

Not alone in meadows and green alleys,
    On the mountain-top, and by the brink
Of sequestered pools in woodland valleys,
    Where the slaves of nature stoop to drink;

FLOWERS

Not alone in her vast dome of glory,
   Not on graves of bird and beast alone,
But in old cathedrals, high and hoary,
   On the tombs of heroes, carved in stone;

In the cottage of the rudest peasant,
   In ancestral homes, whose crumbling towers,
Speaking of the Past unto the Present,
   Tell us of the ancient Games of Flowers;

In all places, then, and in all seasons,
   Flowers expand their light and soul-like wings,
Teaching us, by most persuasive reasons,
   How akin they are to human things.

And with childlike, credulous affection,
   We behold their tender buds expand;
Emblems of our own great resurrection,
   Emblems of the bright and better land.

BALLADS
AND
OTHER POEM

AN APRIL DAY

WHEN the warm sun, that brings
Seed-time and harvest, has returned again,
'T is sweet to visit the still wood, where springs
    The first flower of the plain.

    I love the season well,
When forest glades are teeming with bright forms,
Nor dark and many-folded clouds foretell
    The coming-on of storms.

    From the earth's loosened mould
The sapling draws its sustenance, and thrives;
Though stricken to the heart with winter's cold,
    The drooping tree revives.

    The softly-warbled song
Comes from the pleasant woods, and colored wings
Glance quick in the bright sun, that moves along
    The forest openings.

13

Its shadows in the hollows of the hills,
    And wide the upland glows.

    And when the eve is born,
In the blue lake the sky, o'er-reaching far
Is hollowed out, and the moon dips her horn
    And twinkles many a star.

    Inverted in the tide
Stand the gray rocks, and trembling shadows
And the fair trees look over, side by side,
    And see themselves below.

    Sweet April! many a thought
Is wedded unto thee, as hearts are wed;
Nor shall they fail, till, to its autumn brough
    Life's golden fruit is shed.

WOODS IN WINTER

When winter winds are piercing chill,
　　And through the hawthorn blows the gale,
With solemn feet I tread the hill,
　　That overbrows the lonely vale.

O'er the bare upland, and away
　　Through the long reach of desert woods,
The embracing sunbeams chastely play,
　　And gladden these deep solitudes.

Where, twisted round the barren oak
　　The summer vine in beauty clung,
And summer winds the stillness broke,
　　The crystal icicle is hung.

Where, from their frozen urns, mute springs
　　Pour out the river's gradual tide,
Shrilly the skater's iron rings,
　　And voices fill the woodland side.

Alas! how changed from the fairy scene,
　　When birds sang out their mellow lay,
And winds were soft, and woods were green,
　　And the song ceased not with the day!

Pale, desert woods ! within your crowd ;
And gathering winds, in hoarse accord,
　　Amid the vocal reeds pipe loud.

Chill airs and wintry winds ! my ear
　　Has grown familiar with your song ;
I hear it in the opening year,
　　I listen, and it cheers me long.

"Speak! speak! thou fearful guest!
  Who, with thy hollow breast
  Still in rude armor drest,
    Comest to daunt me!
  Wrapt not in Eastern balms,
  But with thy fleshless palms
  Stretched, as if asking alms,
    Why dost thou haunt me?"

  Then, from those cavernous eyes
  Pale flashes seemed to rise,
  As when the Northern skies
    Gleam in December;
  And, like the water's flow
  Under December's snow,
  Came a dull voice of woe
    From the heart's chamber.

"I was a Viking old!
  My deeds, though manifold,
  No Skald in song has told,
    No Saga taught thee!
  Take heed, that in thy verse
  Thou dost the tale rehearse,
  Else dread a dead man's curse;
    For this I sought thee.

17

"Oft to his frozen lair
  Tracked I the grisly bear,
  While from my path the hare
    Fled like a shadow ;
  Oft through the forest dark
  Followed the were-wolf's bark,
  Until the soaring lark
    Sang from the meadow.

"But when I older grew,
  Joining a corsair's crew,
  O'er the dark sea I flew
    With the marauders.
  Wild was the life we led ;
  Many the souls that sped,
  Many the hearts that bled,
    By our stern orders.

"Many a wassail-bout
  Wore the long Winter out ;

Often our midnight shout
  Set the cocks crowing,
As we the Berserk's tale
Measured in cups of ale,
Draining the oaken pail,
  Filled to o'erflowing.

"Once as I told in glee
  Tales of the stormy sea,
Soft eyes did gaze on me,
  Burning yet tender;
And as the white stars shine
On the dark Norway pine,
On that dark heart of mine
  Fell their soft splendor.

I wooed the blue-eyed maid,
Yielding, yet half afraid,
And in the forest shade
  Our vows were plighted.
Under its loosened vest
Fluttered her little breast,
Like birds within their nest
  By the hawk frighted.

"Bright in her father's hall
  Shields gleamed upon the wall,
Loud sang the minstrels all,
  Chanting his glory;

19

When of old Hildebrand
I asked his daughter's hand,
Mute did the minstrels stand
   To hear my story.

" While the brown ale he quaffed,
Loud then the champion laughed,
And as the wind-gusts waft
   The sea-foam brightly,
So the loud laugh of scorn,
Out of those lips unshorn,
From the deep drinking-horn
   Blew the foam lightly.

"She was a Prince's child,
I but a Viking wild,
And though she blushed and smiled,
   I was discarded!
Should not the dove so white
Follow the sea-mew's flight,
Why did they leave that night
   Her nest unguarded?

"Scarce had I put to sea,
Bearing the maid with me,
Fairest of all was she
   Among the Norsemen!
When on the white sea-strand
Waving his armèd hand,

Saw we old Hildebrand,
    With twenty horsemen.

" Then launched they to the blast,
    Bent like a reed each mast,
    Yet we were gaining fast,
        When the wind failed us ;
    And with a sudden flaw
    Came round the gusty Skaw,
    So that our foe we saw
        Laugh as he hailed us.

" And as to catch the gale
    Round veered the flapping sail,
    ' Death ! ' was the helmsman's hail,
        ' Death without quarter ! '
    Mid-ships with iron keel
    Struck we her ribs of steel ;
    Down her black hulk did reel
        Through the black water !

" As with his wings aslant,
    Sails the fierce cormorant,
    Seeking some rocky haunt,
        With his prey laden, —
    So toward the open main,
    Beating to sea again,
    Through the wild hurricane,
        Bore I the maiden.

"'Three weeks we westward bore,
And when the storm was o'er,
Cloud-like we saw the shore
   Stretching to leeward;
There for my lady's bower
Built I the lofty tower,
Which, to this very hour,
   Stands looking seaward.

"'There lived we many years;
Time dried the maiden's tears;
She had forgot her fears,
   She was a mother;
Death closed her mild blue eyes,
Under that tower she lies;
Ne'er shall the sun arise
   On such another!

"'Still grew my bosom then,
Still as a stagnant fen!
Hateful to me were men,
   The sunlight hateful!
In the vast forest here,
Clad in my warlike gear,
Fell I upon my spear,
   Oh, death was grateful!

"'Thus, seamed with many scars,
Bursting these prison bars,

Up to its native stars
   My soul ascended!
There from the flowing bowl
Deep drinks the warrior's soul,
Skoal! to the Northland! *skoal!*"
   Thus the tale ended.

THE WRECK OF THE HESPERUS

IT was the schooner Hesperus,
　　That sailed the wintry sea;
And the skipper had taken his little daughtèr,
　　To bear him company.

Blue were her eyes as the fairy-flax,
　　Her cheeks like the dawn of day,
And her bosom white as the hawthorn buds,
　　That ope in the month of May.

The skipper he stood beside the helm,
　　His pipe was in his mouth,
And he watched how the veering flaw did blow
　　The smoke now West, now South.

Then up and spake an old Sailòr,
　　Had sailed to the Spanish Main,
"I pray thee, put into yonder port,
　　For I fear a hurricane.

"Last night, the moon had a golden ring,
　　And to-night no moon we see!"
The skipper, he blew a whiff from his pipe,
　　And a scornful laugh laughed he.

He wrapped her warm in his seaman's coat
Against the stinging blast

Colder and louder blew the wind,
　　A gale from the Northeast,
The snow fell hissing in the brine,
　　And the billows frothed like yeast.

Down came the storm, and smote amain
　　The vessel in its strength;
She shuddered and paused, like a frighted steed,
　　Then leaped her cable's length.

"Come hither! come hither! my little daughter,
　　And do not tremble so;
For I can weather the roughest gale
　　That ever wind did blow."

He wrapped her warm in his seaman's coat
　　Against the stinging blast;
He cut a rope from a broken spar,
　　And bound her to the mast.

"O father! I hear the church-bells ring,
　　Oh say, what may it be?"
"'T is a fog-bell on a rock-bound coast!" —
　　And he steered for the open sea.

"O father! I hear the sound of guns,
　　Oh say, what may it be?"
"Some ship in distress, that cannot live
　　In such an angry sea!"

"O father! I see a gleaming light,
    Oh say, what may it be?"
But the father answered never a word,
    A frozen corpse was he.

Lashed to the helm, all stiff and stark,
    With his face turned to the skies,
The lantern gleamed through the gleaming snow
    On his fixed and glassy eyes.

Then the maiden clasped her hands and prayed
    That savèd she might be;
And she thought of Christ, who stilled the wave,
    On the Lake of Galilee.

And fast through the midnight dark and drear,
    Through the whistling sleet and snow,
Like a sheeted ghost, the vessel swept
    Tow'rds the reef of Norman's Woe.

And ever the fitful gusts between
    A sound came from the land;
It was the sound of the trampling surf
    On the rocks and the hard sea-sand.

The breakers were right beneath her bows,
    She drifted a dreary wreck,
And a whooping billow swept the crew
    Like icicles from her deck.

She struck where the white and fleecy waves
    Looked soft as carded wool,
But the cruel rocks, they gored her side
    Like the horns of an angry bull.

Her rattling shrouds, all sheathed in ice,
    With the masts went by the board;
Like a vessel of glass, she stove and sank,
    Ho! ho! the breakers roared!

At daybreak, on the bleak sea-beach,
    A fisherman stood aghast,
To see the form of a maiden fair,
    Lashed close to a drifting mast.

The salt sea was frozen on her breast,
    The salt tears in her eyes;
And he saw her hair, like the brown sea-weed,
    On the billows fall and rise.

Such was the wreck of the Hesperus
    In the midnight and the snow!
Christ save us all from a death like this,
    On the reef of Norman's Woe!

THE VILLAGE BLACKSMITH

Under a spreading chestnut-tree
The village smithy stands;
The smith, a mighty man is he,
With large and sinewy hands;
And the muscles of his brawny arms
Are strong as iron bands.

His hair is crisp, and black, and long,
His face is like the tan;
His brow is wet with honest sweat,
He earns whate'er he can,
And looks the whole world in the face,
For he owes not any man.

Week in, week out, from morn till night,
You can hear his bellows blow;
You can hear him swing his heavy sledge,
With measured beat and slow,
Like a sexton ringing the village bell,
When the evening sun is low.

And children coming home from school
Look in at the open door;
They love to see the flaming forge,
And hear the bellows roar,

And catch the burning sparks that fly
　　Like chaff from a threshing-floor.

He goes on Sunday to the church,
　　And sits among his boys;
He hears the parson pray and preach,
　　He hears his daughter's voice,
Singing in the village choir,
　　And it makes his heart rejoice.

It sounds to him like her mother's voice,
　　Singing in Paradise!
He needs must think of her once more
　　How in the grave she lies;
And with his hard, rough hand he wipes
　　A tear out of his eyes.

Toiling, — rejoicing, — sorrowing,
　　Onward through life he goes;
Each morning sees some task begin,
　　Each evening sees it close;
Something attempted, something done,
　　Has earned a night's repose.

Thanks, thanks to thee, my worthy friend,
　　For the lesson thou hast taught!
Thus at the flaming forge of life
　　Our fortunes must be wrought;
Thus on its sounding anvil shaped
　　Each burning deed and thought.

IT IS NOT ALWAYS MAY

THE sun is bright, — the air is clear,
　The darting swallows soar and sing,
And from the stately elms I hear
　The bluebird prophesying Spring.

So blue yon winding river flows,
　It seems an outlet from the sky,
Where, waiting till the west wind blows,
　The freighted clouds at anchor lie.

All things are new ; — the buds, the leaves,
　That gild the elm-tree's nodding crest,
And even the nest beneath the eaves ; —
　There are no birds in last year's nest !

All things rejoice in youth and love
　The fulness of their first delight !
And learn from the soft heavens above
　The melting tenderness of night.

Maiden, that read'st this simple rhyme,
　Enjoy thy youth, it will not stay ;
Enjoy the fragrance of thy prime,
　For oh, it is not always May !

Enjoy the Spring of Love and Youth,
  To some good angel leave the rest;
For Time will teach thee soon the truth,
  There are no birds in last year s nest!

TO THE RIVER CHARLES

River! that in silence windest
  Through the meadows, bright and free,
Till at length thy rest thou findest
  In the bosom of the sea!

Four long years of mingled feeling,
  Half in rest, and half in strife,
I have seen thy waters stealing
  Onward, like the stream of life.

Thou hast taught me, Silent River!
  Many a lesson, deep and long;
Thou hast been a generous giver;
  I can give thee but a song.

Oft in sadness and in illness,
  I have watched thy current glide,
Till the beauty of its stillness
  Overflowed me, like a tide.

And in better hours and brighter,
  When I saw thy waters gleam,
I have felt my heart beat lighter,
  And leap onward with thy stream.

Not for this alone I love thee,
  Nor because thy waves of blue
From celestial seas above thee
  Take their own celestial hue.

Where yon shadowy woodlands hide thee,
  And thy waters disappear,
Friends I love have dwelt beside thee,
  And have made thy margin dear.

More than this; — thy name reminds me
  Of three friends, all true and tried;
And that name, like magic, binds me
  Closer, closer to thy side.

Friends my soul with joy remembers!
  How like quivering flames they start,
When I fan the living embers
  On the hearth-stone of my heart!

'T is for this, thou Silent River!
  That my spirit leans to thee;
Thou hast been a generous giver,
  Take this idle song from me.

MAIDENHOOD

Maiden! with the meek, brown eyes,
In whose orbs a shadow lies
Like the dusk in evening skies!

Thou whose locks outshine the sun,
Golden tresses, wreathed in one,
As the braided streamlets run!

Standing, with reluctant feet,
Where the brook and river meet
Womanhood and childhood fleet!

Gazing, with a timid glance,
On the brooklet's swift advance,
On the river's broad expanse!

Deep and still, that gliding stream
Beautiful to thee must seem,
As the river of a dream.

Then why pause with indecision,
When bright angels in thy vision
Beckon thee to fields Elysian?

Seest thou shadows sailing by,
As the dove, with startled eye,
Sees the falcon's shadow fly?

Hearest thou voices on the shore,
That our ears perceive no more,
Deafened by the cataract's roar?

Oh, thou child of many prayers!
Life hath quicksands, — Life hath snares!
Care and age come unawares!

Like the swell of some sweet tune,
Morning rises into noon
May glides onward into June.

Childhood is the bough, where slumbered
Birds and blossoms many-numbered; —
Age, that bough with snows encumbered.

Gather, then, each flower that grows,
When the young heart overflows,
To embalm that tent of snows.

Bear a lily in thy hand;
Gates of brass cannot withstand
One touch of that magic wand.

Bear through sorrow, wrong, and ruth,
In thy heart the dew of youth,
On thy lips the smile of truth.

And that smile, like sunshine, dart
Into many a sunless heart,
For a smile of God thou art.

EXCELSIOR

THE shades of night were falling fast,
As through an Alpine village passed
A youth, who bore, 'mid snow and ice,
A banner with the strange device,
　　　　Excelsior!

His brow was sad ; his eye beneath
Flashed like a falchion from its sheath,
And like a silver clarion rung
The accents of that unknown tongue,
　　　　Excelsior!

In happy homes he saw the light
Of household fires gleam warm and bright;
Above, the spectral glaciers shone,
And from his lips escaped a groan,
　　　　Excelsior!

"Try not the Pass!" the old man said;
"Dark lowers the tempest overhead,
The roaring torrent is deep and wide!"
And loud that clarion voice replied,
　　　　Excelsior!

"Oh stay," the maiden said, "and rest
Thy weary head upon this breast!"
A tear stood in his bright blue eye,
But still he answered, with a sigh,
Excelsior!

"Beware the pine-tree's withered branch!
Beware the awful avalanche!"
This was the peasant's last Good-night;
A voice replied, far up the height,
Excelsior!

At break of day, as heavenward
The pious monks of Saint Bernard
Uttered the oft-repeated prayer,
A voice cried through the startled air,
Excelsior!

A traveller, by the faithful hound,
Half-buried in the snow was found
Still grasping in his hand of ice
That banner with the strange device
Excelsior!

There in the twilight cold and gray,
Lifeless, but beautiful, he lay,
And from the sky, serene and far,
A voice fell, like a falling star,
Excelsior!

THE SLAVE'S DREAM

BESIDE the ungathered rice he lay,
    His sickle in his hand;
His breast was bare, his matted hair
    Was buried in the sand.
Again, in the mist and shadow of sleep,
    He saw his Native Land.

Wide through the landscape of his dreams
    The lordly Niger flowed;
Beneath the palm-trees on the plain
    Once more a king he strode;
And heard the tinkling caravans
    Descend the mountain road.

He saw once more his dark-eyed queen
    Among her children stand;
They clasped his neck, they kissed his cheeks,
    They held him by the hand! —
A tear burst from the sleeper's lids
    And fell into the sand.

And then at furious speed he rode
    Along the Niger's bank;
His bridle-reins were golden chains,
    And, with a martial clank,

At each leap he could feel his scabbard of steel
   Smiting his stallion's flank.

Before him, like a blood-red flag,
   The bright flamingoes flew ;
From morn till night he followed their flight,
   O'er plains where the tamarind grew,
Till he saw the roofs of Caffre huts,
   And the ocean rose to view.

At night he heard the lion roar,
   And the hyena scream,
And the river-horse, as he crushed the reeds
   Beside some hidden stream ;
And it passed, like a glorious roll of drums,
   Through the triumph of his dream.

The forests, with their myriad tongues,
   Shouted of liberty ;
And the Blast of the Desert cried aloud,
   With a voice so wild and free,
That he started in his sleep and smiled
   At their tempestuous glee.

He did not feel the driver's whip,
   Nor the burning heat of day;
For Death had illumined the Land of Sleep,
   And his lifeless body lay
A worn-out fetter, that the soul
   Had broken and thrown away !

THE SLAVE IN THE DISMAL SWAMP

In dark fens of the Dismal Swamp
   The hunted Negro lay;
He saw the fire of the midnight camp,
And heard at times a horse's tramp
   And a bloodhound's distant bay.

Where will-o'-the-wisps and glow-worms shine,
   In bulrush and in brake;
Where waving mosses shroud the pine,
And the cedar grows, and the poisonous vine
   Is spotted like the snake;

Where hardly a human foot could pass,
   Or a human heart would dare,
On the quaking turf of the green morass
He crouched in the rank and tangled grass,
   Like a wild beast in his lair.

A poor old slave, infirm and lame;
   Great scars deformed his face;
On his forehead he bore the brand of shame,
And the rags, that hid his mangled frame,
   Were the livery of disgrace.

All things above were bright and fair,
   All things were glad and free;

Lithe squirrels darted here and there,
And wild birds filled the echoing air
　With songs of Liberty !

On him alone was the doom of pain,
　From the morning of his birth;
On him alone the curse of Cain
Fell, like a flail on the garnered grain;
　And struck him to the earth !

SERENADE

FROM "THE SPANISH STUDENT"

STARS of the summer night!
    Far in yon azure deeps,
Hide, hide your golden light!
    She sleeps!
My lady sleeps!
    Sleeps!

Moon of the summer night!
    Far down yon western steeps,
Sink, sink in silver light!
    She sleeps!
My lady sleeps!
    Sleeps!

Wind of the summer night!
    Where yonder woodbine creeps,
Fold, fold thy pinions light!
    She sleeps!
My lady sleeps!
    Sleeps!

Dreams of the summer night!
    Tell her, her lover keeps
Watch! while in slumbers light
    She sleeps!
My lady sleeps!
    Sleeps!

THE BELFRY OF BRUGES
AND OTHER POEMS

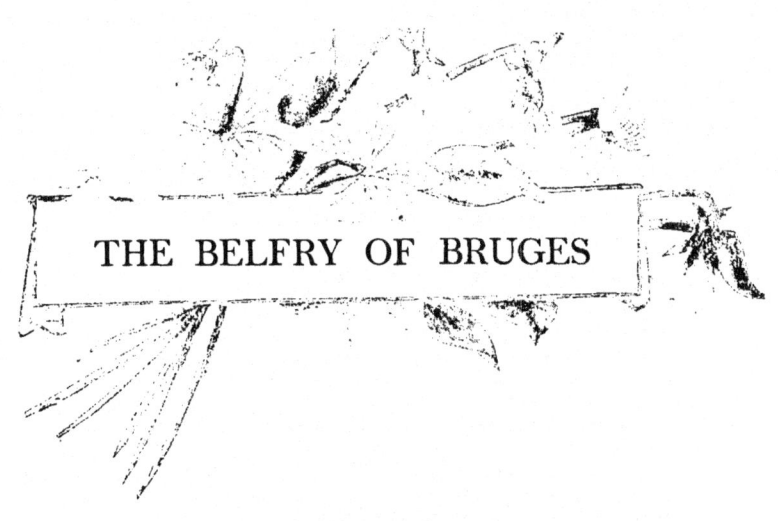

THE BELFRY OF BRUGES

CARILLON

In the ancient town of Bruges,
In the quaint old Flemish city,
As the evening shades descended,
Low and loud and sweetly blended,
Low at times and loud at times,
And changing like a poet's rhymes,
Rang the beautiful wild chimes
From the Belfry in the market
Of the ancient town of Bruges.

Then, with deep sonorous clangor
Calmly answering their sweet anger,
When the wrangling bells had ended,
Slowly struck the clock eleven
And, from out the silent heaven,
Silence on the town descended.
Silence, silence everywhere,
On the earth and in the air,
Save that footsteps here and there

Of some burgher home returning,
Bv the street lamps faintly burning,
For a moment woke the echoes
Of the ancient town of Bruges.

But amid my broken slumbers
Still I heard those magic numbers,
As they loud proclaimed the flight
And stolen marches of the night;
Till their chimes in sweet collision
Mingled with each wandering vision,
Mingled with the fortune-telling
Gypsy-bands of dreams and fancies,
Which amid the waste expanses
Of the silent land of trances
Have their solitary dwelling;
All else seemed asleep in Bruges,
In the quaint old Flemish city.

And I thought how like these chimes
Are the poet's airy rhymes,
All his rhymes and roundelays,
His conceits, and songs, and ditties,
From the belfry of his brain,
Scattered downward, though in vain,
On the roofs and stones of cities!
For by night the drowsy ear
Under its curtains cannot hear,
And by day men go their ways,

Hearing the music as they pass,
But deeming it no more, alas!
Than the hollow sound of brass.

Yet perchance a sleepless wight,
Lodging at some humble inn
In the narrow lanes of life,
When the dusk and hush of night
Shut out the incessant din
Of daylight and its toil and strife,
May listen with a calm delight
To the poet's melodies,
Till he hears, or dreams he hears,
Intermingled with the song,
Thoughts that he has cherished long;
Hears amid the chime and singing
The bells of his own village ringing,
And wakes, and finds his slumberous eyes
Wet with most delicious tears.

Thus dreamed I, as by night I lay
In Bruges, at the Fleur-de-Blé,
Listening with a wild delight
To the chimes that, through the night,
Rang their changes from the Belfry
Of that quaint old Flemish city.

THE BELFRY OF BRUGES

In the market-place of Bruges stands the belfry old and
  brown;
Thrice consumed and thrice rebuilded, still it watches
  o'er the town.

As the summer morn was breaking, on that lofty tower
  I stood,
And the world threw off the darkness, like the weeds of
  widowhood.

Thick with towns and hamlets studded, and with
  streams and vapors gray,
Like a shield embossed with silver, round and vast the
  landscape lay.

At my feet the city slumbered. From its chimneys, here
  and there,
Wreaths of snow-white smoke, ascending, vanished,
  ghost-like, into air.

Not a sound rose from the city at that early morning
  hour,
But I heard a heart of iron beating in the ancient tower.

From their nests beneath the rafters sang the swallows
    wild and high;
And the world, beneath me sleeping, seemed more dis-
    tant than the sky

Then most musical and solemn, bringing back the olden
    times,
With their strange, unearthly changes rang the melan-
    choly chimes,

Like the psalms from some old cloister, when the nuns
    sing in the choir;
And the great bell tolled among them, like the chanting
    of a friar.

Visions of the days departed, shadowy phantoms filled
    my brain;
They who live in history only seemed to walk the earth
    again;

All the Foresters of Flanders, — mighty Baldwin Bras
    de Fer,
Lyderick du Bucq and Cressy, Philip, Guy de Dam-
    pierre.

I beheld the pageants splendid that adorned those days
    of old;
Stately dames, like queens attended, knights who bore
    the Fleece of Gold;

Lombard and Venetian merchants with deep-laden
    argosies;
Ministers from twenty nations; more than royal pomp
    and ease.

I beheld proud Maximilian, kneeling humbly on the
    ground;
I beheld the gentle Mary, hunting with her hawk and
    hound;

And her lighted bridal-chamber, where a duke slept
    with the queen,
And the armèd guard around them, and the sword
    unsheathed between.

I beheld the Flemish weavers, with Namur and Juliers
    bold,
Marching homeward from the bloody battle of the Spurs
    of Gold;

Saw the fight at Minnewater, saw the White Hoods
    moving west,
Saw great Artevelde victorious scale the Golden Drag-
    on's nest.

And again the whiskered Spaniard all the land with
    terror smote;
And again the wild alarum sounded from the tocsin's
    throat;

Till the bell of Ghent responded o'er lagoon and dike of
    sand,
"I am Roland! I am Roland! there is victory in the
    land!"

Then the sound of drums aroused me. The awakened
    city's roar
Chased the phantoms I had summoned back into their
    graves once more.

Hours had passed away like minutes; and, before I was
    aware,
Lo! the shadow of the belfry crossed the sun-illumined
    square.

THE ARSENAL AT SPRINGFIELD

This is the Arsenal. From floor to ceiling,
  Like a huge organ, rise the burnished arms;
But from their silent pipes no anthem pealing
  Startles the villages with strange alarms.

Ah! what a sound will rise, how wild and dreary,
  When the death-angel touches those swift keys!
What loud lament and dismal Miserere
  Will mingle with their awful symphonies!

I hear even now the infinite fierce chorus,
  The cries of agony, the endless groan,
Which, through the ages that have gone before us,
  In long reverberations reach our own.

On helm and harness rings the Saxon hammer,
  Through Cimbric forest roars the Norseman's song,
And loud, amid the universal clamor,
  O'er distant deserts sounds the Tartar gong.

I hear the Florentine, who from his palace
  Wheels out his battle-bell with dreadful din,
And Aztec priests upon their teocallis
  Beat the wild war-drums made of serpent's skin;

54

The tumult of each sacked and burning village;
   The shout that every prayer for mercy drowns;
The soldiers' revels in the midst of pillage;
   The wail of famine in beleaguered towns;

The bursting shell, the gateway wrenched asunder,
   The rattling musketry, the clashing blade;
And ever and anon, in tones of thunder
   The diapason of the cannonade.

Is it, O man, with such discordant noises,
   With such accursed instruments as these,
Thou drownest Nature's sweet and kindly voices,
   And jarrest the celestial harmonies?

Were half the power that fills the world with terror,
   Were half the wealth bestowed on camps and courts,
Given to redeem the human mind from error
   There were no need of arsenals or forts:

The warrior's name would be a name abhorrèd!
   And every nation, that should lift again
Its hand against a brother, on its forehead
   Would wear forevermore the curse of Cain!

Down the dark future, through long generations,
   The echoing sounds grow fainter and then cease;
And like a bell, with solemn, sweet vibrations,
   I hear once more the voice of Christ say, "Peace!"

Peace! and no longer from its brazen portals
   The blast of War's great organ shakes the skies!
But beautiful as songs of the immortals,
   The holy melodies of love arise.

THE NORMAN BARON

In his chamber, weak and dying,
Was the Norman baron lying;
Loud, without, the tempest thundered,
    And the castle-turret shook.

In this fight was Death the gainer
Spite of vassal and retainer,
And the lands his sires had plundered,
    Written in the Doomsday Book.

By his bed a monk was seated,
Who in humble voice repeated
Many a prayer and pater-noster,
    From the missal on his knee;

And, amid the tempest pealing,
Sounds of bells came faintly stealing,
Bells, that from the neighboring kloster
    Rang for the Nativity.

In the hall, the serf and vassal
Held, that night, their Christmas wassail;
Many a carol, old and saintly,
    Sang the minstrels and the waits;

And so loud these Saxon gleemen
Sang to slaves the songs of freemen,
That the storm was heard but faintly,
    Knocking at the castle-gates.

Till at length the lays they chanted
Reached the chamber terror-haunted,
Where the monk, with accents holy,
    Whispered at the baron's ear.

Tears upon his eyelids glistened,
As he paused awhile and listened,
And the dying baron slowly
    Turned his weary head to hear.

Wassail for the kingly stranger
Born and cradled in a manger!
King, like David, priest, like Aaron,
    Christ is born to set us free!"

And the lightning showed the sainted
Figures on the casement painted,
And exclaimed the shuddering baron,
    "Miserere, Domine!"

In that hour of deep contrition
He beheld, with clearer vision,
Through all outward show and fashion,
    Justice, the Avenger, rise.

All the pomp of earth had vanished,
Falsehood and deceit were banished,
Reason spake more loud than passion,
    And the truth wore no disguise.

Every vassal of his banner,
Every serf born to his manor,
All those wronged and wretched creatures,
    By his hand were freed again.

And, as on the sacred missal
He recorded their dismissal,
Death relaxed his iron features,
    And the monk replied, "Amen!"

Many centuries have been numbered
Since in death the baron slumbered
By the convent's sculptured portal,
    Mingling with the common dust:

But the good deed, through the ages
Living in historic pages,
Brighter grows and gleams immortal,
    Unconsumed by moth or rust.

RAIN IN SUMMER

How beautiful is the rain!
After the dust and heat,
In the broad and fiery street,
In the narrow lane,
How beautiful is the rain!

How it clatters along the roofs,
Like the tramp of hoofs!
How it gushes and struggles out
From the throat of the overflowing spout!

Across the window-pane
It pours and pours;
And swift and wide,
With a muddy tide,
Like a river down the gutter roars
The rain, the welcome rain!

The sick man from his chamber looks
At the twisted brooks;
He can feel the cool
Breath of each little pool;
His fevered brain
Grows calm again,
And he breathes a blessing on the rain.

From the neighboring school
Come the boys,
With more than their wonted noise
And commotion;
And down the wet streets
Sail their mimic fleets,
Till the treacherous pool
Ingulfs them in its whirling
And turbulent ocean.

In the country, on every side,
Where far and wide,
Like a leopard's tawny and spotted hide,
Stretches the plain,
To the dry grass and the drier grain
How welcome is the rain!

In the furrowed land
The toilsome and patient oxen stand;
Lifting the yoke-encumbered head,
With their dilated nostrils spread,
They silently inhale
The clover-scented gale,
And the vapors that arise
From the well-watered and smoking soil.
For this rest in the furrow after toil
Their large and lustrous eyes
Seem to thank the Lord,
More than man's spoken word.

Near at hand,
From under the sheltering trees,
The farmer sees
His pastures, and his fields of grain
As they bend their tops
To the numberless beating drops
Of the incessant rain.
He counts it as no sin
That he sees therein
Only his own thrift and gain.

These, and far more than these,
The Poet sees!
He can behold
Aquarius old
Walking the fenceless fields of air;
And from each ample fold
Of the clouds about him rolled
Scattering everywhere
The showery rain,
As the farmer scatters his grain.

He can behold
Things manifold
That have not yet been wholly told, —
Have not been wholly sung nor said.
For his thought, that never stops,
Follows the water-drops
Down to the graves of the dead,

Down through chasms and gulfs profound,
To the dreary fountain-head
Of lakes and rivers under ground;
And sees them, when the rain is done,
On the bridge of colors seven
Climbing up once more to heaven,
Opposite the setting sun.

Thus the Seer
With vision clear,
Sees forms appear and disappear,
In the perpetual round of strange,
Mysterious change
From birth to death, from death to birth,
From earth to heaven, from heaven to earth;
Till glimpses more sublime
Of things unseen before,
Unto his wondering eyes reveal
The Universe, as an immeasurable wheel
Turning forevermore
In the rapid and rushing river of Time.

THE BRIDGE

I stood on the bridge at midnight,
  As the clocks were striking the hour,
And the moon rose o'er the city,
  Behind the dark church-tower.

I saw her bright reflection
  In the waters under me,
Like a golden goblet falling
  And sinking into the sea.

And far in the hazy distance
  Of that lovely night in June,
The blaze of the flaming furnace
  Gleamed redder than the moon.

Among the long, black rafters
  The wavering shadows lay,
And the current that came from the ocean
  Seemed to lift and bear them away;

As, sweeping and eddying through them,
  Rose the belated tide,
And, streaming into the moonlight,
  The seaweed floated wide.

And like those waters rushing
  Among the wooden piers,
A flood of thoughts came o'er me
  That filled my eyes with tears.

How often, oh how often,
  In the days that had gone by,
I had stood on that bridge at midnight
  And gazed on that wave and sky!

How often, oh how often,
  I had wished that the ebbing tide
Would bear me away on its bosom
  O'er the ocean wild and wide!

For my heart was hot and restless,
  And my life was full of care,
And the burden laid upon me
  Seemed greater than I could bear.

But now it has fallen from me,
  It is buried in the sea;
And only the sorrow of others
  Throws its shadow over me.

Yet whenever I cross the river
  On its bridge with wooden piers,
Like the odor of brine from the ocean
  Comes the thought of other years.

And I think how many thousands
Of care-encumbered men,
Each bearing his burden of sorrow,
Have crossed the bridge since then.

I see the long procession
Still passing to and fro,
The young heart hot and restless,
And the old subdued and slow!

And forever and forever
As long as the river flows,
As long as the heart has passions,
As long as life has woes;

The moon and its broken reflection
And its shadows shall appear,
As the symbol of love in heaven,
And its wavering image here.

THE DAY IS DONE

THE day is done, and the darkness
    Falls from the wings of Night,
As a feather is wafted downward
    From an eagle in his flight.

I see the lights of the village
    Gleam through the rain and the mist,
And a feeling of sadness comes o er me
    That my soul cannot resist:

A feeling of sadness and longing,
    That is not akin to pain,
And resembles sorrow only
    As the mist resembles the rain.

Come, read to me some poem
    Some simple and heartfelt lay
That shall soothe this restless feeling,
    And banish the thoughts of day.

Not from the grand old masters,
    Not from the bards sublime,
Whose distant footsteps echo
    Through the corridors of Time.

For, like strains of martial music,
  Their mighty thoughts suggest
Life's endless toil and endeavor;
  And to-night I long for rest.

Read from some humbler poet,
  Whose songs gushed from his heart,
As showers from the clouds of summer,
  Or tears from the eyelids start;

Who, through long days of labor,
  And nights devoid of ease,
Still heard in his soul the music
  Of wonderful melodies.

Such songs have power to quiet
  The restless pulse of care,
And come like the benediction
  That follows after prayer.

Then read from the treasured volume
  The poem of thy choice,
And lend to the rhyme of the poet
  The beauty of thy voice.

And the night shall be filled with music,
  And the cares, that infest the day,
Shall fold their tents, like the Arabs,
  And as silently steal away.

TO THE DRIVING CLOUD

Gloomy and dark art thou, O chief of the mighty
    Omahas ;
Gloomy and dark as the driving cloud, whose name
    thou hast taken !
Wrapped in thy scarlet blanket, I see thee stalk through
    the city's
Narrow and populous streets, as once by the margin of
    rivers
Stalked those birds unknown, that have left us only
    their footprints.
What, in a few short years, will remain of thy race but
    the footprints ?

How canst thou walk these streets, who hast trod the
    green turf of the prairies ?
How canst thou breathe this air, who hast breathed the
    sweet air of the mountains ?
Ah ! 't is in vain that with lordly looks of disdain thou
    dost challenge
Looks of disdain in return, and question these walls and
    these pavements,
Claiming the soil for thy hunting-grounds, while down-
    trodden millions
Starve in the garrets of Europe, and cry from its caverns
    that they, too,
Have been created heirs of the earth, and claim its divi-
    sion !

Back, then, back to thy woods in the regions west of
    the Wabash !
There as a monarch thou reignest. In autumn the leaves
    of the maple
Pave the floors of thy palace-halls with gold, and in
    summer
Pine-trees waft through its chambers the odorous breath
    of their branches.
There thou art strong and great, a hero, a tamer of
    horses !
There thou chasest the stately stag on the banks of the
    Elkhorn,
Or by the roar of the Running-Water, or where the
    Omaha
Calls thee, and leaps through the wild ravine like a brave
    of the Blackfeet !

Hark ! what murmurs arise from the heart of those
    mountainous deserts ?
Is it the cry of the Foxes and Crows, or the mighty
    Behemoth,
Who, unharmed, on his tusks once caught the bolts of
    the thunder,
And now lurks in his lair to destroy the race of the red
    man ?
Far more fatal to thee and thy race than the Crows and
    the Foxes,
Far more fatal to thee and thy race than the tread of
    Behemoth,

Lo! the big thunder-canoe, that steadily breasts the
  Missouri's
Merciless current ! and yonder, afar on the prairies, the
  camp-fires
Gleam through the night ; and the cloud of dust in the
  gray of the daybreak
Marks not the buffalo's track, nor the Mandan's dex-
  terous horse-race ;
It is a caravan, whitening the desert where dwell the
  Camanches !
Ha ! how the breath of these Saxons and Celts, like the
  blast of the east-wind,
Drifts evermore to the west the scanty smokes of thy
  wigwams !

WALTER VON DER VOGELWEID

Vogelweid the Minnesinger,
  When he left this world of ours,
Laid his body in the cloister,
  Under Würtzburg's minster towers.

And he gave the monks his treasures,
  Gave them all with this behest:
They should feed the birds at noontide
  Daily on his place of rest;

Saying, "From these wandering minstrels
  I have learned the art of song;
Let me now repay the lessons
  They have taught so well and long."

Thus the bard of love departed;
  And, fulfilling his desire,
On his tomb the birds were feasted
  By the children of the choir.

Day by day, o'er tower and turret,
  In foul weather and in fair,
Day by day, in vaster numbers,
  Flocked the poets of the air.

On the tree whose heavy branches
  Overshadowed all the place,
On the pavement, on the tombstone,
  On the poet's sculptured face,

On the cross-bars of each window,
  On the lintel of each door,
They renewed the War of Wartburg,
  Which the bard had fought before.

There they sang their merry carols,
  Sang their lauds on every side;
And the name their voices uttered
  Was the name of Vogelweid.

Till at length the portly abbot
  Murmured, "Why this waste of food?
Be it changed to loaves henceforward
  For our fasting brotherhood."

Then in vain o'er tower and turret,
  From the walls and woodland nests,
When the minster bells rang noontide
  Gathered the unwelcome guests.

Then in vain, with cries discordant,
  Clamorous round the Gothic spire,
Screamed the feathered Minnesingers
  For the children of the choir.

Time has long effaced the inscriptions
On the cloister's funeral stones,
And tradition only tells us
Where repose the poet's bones.

But around the vast cathedral,
By sweet echoes multiplied,
Still the birds repeat the legend,
And the name of Vogelweid.

THE OLD CLOCK ON THE STAIRS

Somewhat back from the village street
Stands the old-fashioned country-seat.
Across its antique portico
Tall poplar-trees their shadows throw;
And from its station in the hall
An ancient timepiece says to all, —
   "Forever — never!
      Never — forever!"

Half-way up the stairs it stands,
And points and beckons with its hands
From its case of massive oak,
Like a monk, who, under his cloak,
Crosses himself, and sighs, alas!
With sorrowful voice to all who pass, —
   "Forever — never!
      Never — forever!"

By day its voice is low and light;
But in the silent dead of night,
Distinct as a passing footstep's fall,
It echoes along the vacant hall,
Along the ceiling, along the floor,
And seems to say, at each chamber-door, —
   "Forever — never!
      Never — forever!"

Through days of sorrow and of mirth,
Through days of death and days of birth,
Through every swift vicissitude
Of changeful time, unchanged it has stood,
And as if, like God, it all things saw,
It calmly repeats those words of awe, —
    " Forever — never!
      Never — forever! "

In that mansion used to be
Free-hearted Hospitality;
His great fires up the chimney roared;
The stranger feasted at his board;
But, like the skeleton at the feast,
That warning timepiece never ceased, —
    "Forever — never!
      Never — forever! "

There groups of merry children played,
There youths and maidens dreaming strayed;
O precious hours! O golden prime,
And affluence of love and time!
Even as a miser counts his gold,
Those hours the ancient timepiece told, —
    "Forever — never!
      Never — forever! "

From that chamber, clothed in white,
The bride came forth on her wedding night;

There, in that silent room below,
The dead lay in his shroud of snow;
And in the hush that followed the prayer,
Was heard the old clock on the stair, —
    "Forever — never!
      Never — forever!"

All are scattered now and fled,
Some are married, some are dead;
And when I ask, with throbs of pain,
"Ah! when shall they all meet again?"
As in the days long since gone by,
The ancient timepiece makes reply,
    "Forever — never!
      Never — forever!"

Never here, forever there,
Where all parting, pain, and care,
And death, and time shall disappear, —
Forever there, but never here!
The horologe of Eternity
Sayeth this incessantly, —
    "Forever — never!
      Never — forever!"

THE ARROW AND THE SONG

I SHOT an arrow into the air,
It fell to earth, I knew not where;
For, so swiftly it flew, the sight
Could not follow it in its flight.

I breathed a song into the air,
It fell to earth, I knew not where;
For who has sight so keen and strong,
That it can follow the flight of song?

Long, long afterward, in an oak
I found the arrow, still unbroke;
And the song, from beginning to end,
I found again in the heart of a friend.

CURFEW

Solemnly, mournfully,
  Dealing its dole,
The Curfew Bell
  Is beginning to toll.

Cover the embers,
  And put out the light;
Toil comes with the morning,
  And rest with the night.

Dark grow the windows,
  And quenched is the fire;
Sound fades into silence,—
  All footsteps retire.

No voice in the chambers,
  No sound in the hall!
Sleep and oblivion
  Reign over all!

II

The book is completed,
  And closed, like the day;
And the hand that has written it
  Lays it away.

Dim grow its fancies ;
Forgotten they lie ;
Like coals in the ashes,
They darken and die.

Song sinks into silence,
The story is told,
The windows are darkened,
The hearth-stone is cold.

Darker and darker
The black shadows fall ;
Sleep and oblivion
Reign over all.

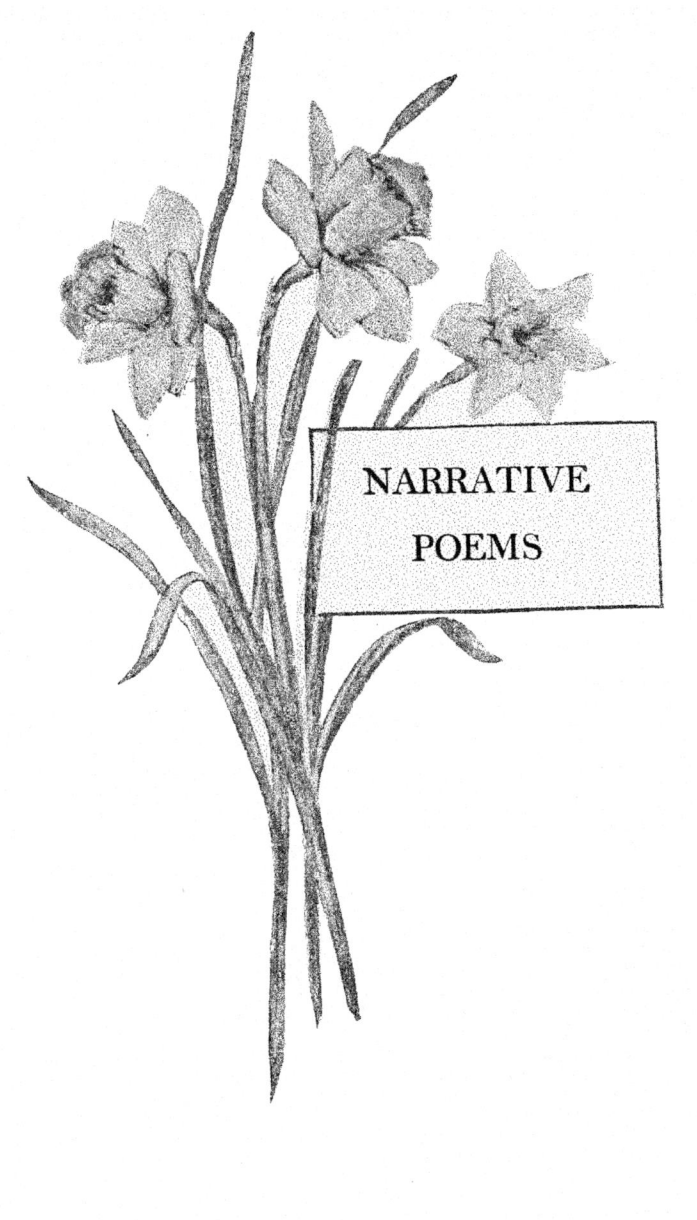

NARRATIVE
POEMS

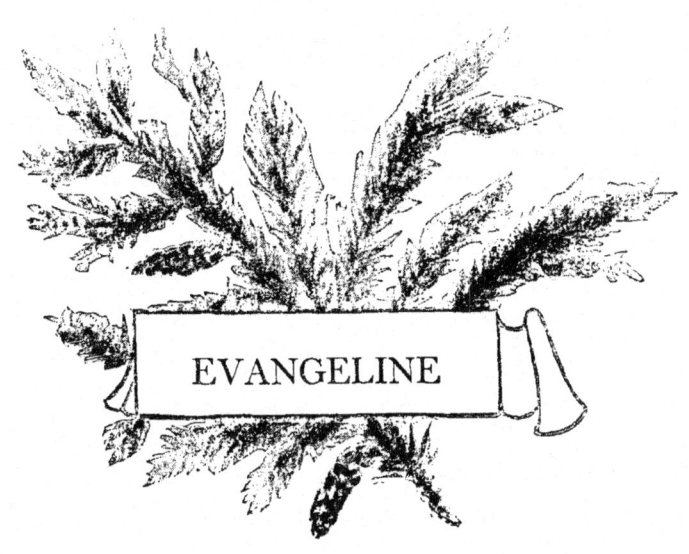

EVANGELINE

THIS is the forest primeval. The murmuring pines and
the hemlocks,
Bearded with moss, and in garments green, indistinct
in the twilight,
Stand like Druids of eld, with voices sad and prophetic,
Stand like harpers hoar, with beards that rest on their
bosoms.
Loud from its rocky caverns, the deep-voiced neighbor-
ing ocean
Speaks, and in accents disconsolate answers the wail of
the forest.

This is the forest primeval ; but where are the hearts
that beneath it
Leaped like the roe, when he hears in the woodland the
voice of the huntsman ?
Where is the thatch-roofed village, the home of Aca-
dian farmers, —
Men whose lives glided on like rivers that water the
woodlands,

Darkened by shadows of earth, but reflecting an image
of heaven?
Waste are those pleasant farms, and the farmers for-
ever departed!
Scattered like dust and leaves, when the mighty blasts
of October
Seize them, and whirl them aloft, and sprinkle them far
o'er the ocean.
Naught but tradition remains of the beautiful village
of Grand-Pré.

Ye who believe in affection that hopes, and endures,
and is patient,
Ye who believe in the beauty and strength of woman's
devotion,
List to the mournful tradition, still sung by the pines of
the forest;
List to a Tale of Love in Acadie, home of the happy.

In the Acadian land, on the shores of the Basin of
    Minas,
Distant, secluded, still, the little village of Grand-Pré
Lay in the fruitful valley. Vast meadows stretched to
    the eastward,
Giving the village its name, and pasture to flocks with-
    out number.
Dikes, that the hands of the farmers had raised with
    labor incessant,
Shut out the turbulent tides ; but at stated seasons the
    flood-gates
Opened, and welcomed the sea to wander at will o'er
    the meadows.
West and south there were fields of flax, and orchards
    and cornfields
Spreading afar and unfenced o'er the plain ; and away
    to the northward
Blomidon rose, and the forests old, and aloft on the
    mountains
Sea-fogs pitched their tents, and mists from the mighty
    Atlantic
Looked on the happy valley, but ne'er from their station
    descended.

There, in the midst of its farms, reposed the Acadian
village.
Strongly built were the houses, with frames of oak and
of hemlock,
Such as the peasants of Normandy built in the reign
of the Henries.
Thatched were the roofs, with dormer-windows ; and
gables projecting
Over the basement below protected and shaded the
doorway.
There in the tranquil evenings of summer, when
brightly the sunset
Lighted the village street, and gilded the vanes on the
chimneys,
Matrons and maidens sat in snow-white caps and in
kirtles
Scarlet and blue and green, with distaffs spinning the
golden
Flax for the gossiping looms, whose noisy shuttles
within doors
Mingled their sounds with the whir of the wheels and
the songs of the maidens.
Solemnly down the street came the parish priest, and
the children
Paused in their play to kiss the hand he extended to
bless them.
Reverend walked he among them ; and up rose matrons
and maidens,

Hailing his slow approach with words of affectionate
welcome.

Then came the laborers home from the field, and se-
renely the sun sank

Down to his rest, and twilight prevailed. Anon from
the belfry

Softly the Angelus sounded, and over the roofs of the
village

Columns of pale blue smoke, like clouds of incense as-
cending,

Rose from a hundred hearths, the homes of peace and
contentment.

Thus dwelt together in love these simple Acadian
farmers, —

Dwelt in the love of God and of man. Alike were they
free from

Fear, that reigns with the tyrant, and envy, the vice of
republics.

Neither locks had they to their doors, nor bars to their
windows ;

But their dwellings were open as day and the hearts of
the owners ;

There the richest was poor, and the poorest lived in
abundance.

Somewhat apart from the village, and nearer the
Basin of Minas,

Benedict Bellefontaine, the wealthiest farmer of Grand-
Pré,

Dwelt on his goodly acres ; and with him, directing his
household,
Gentle Evangeline lived, his child, and the pride of the
village.
Stalworth and stately in form was the man of seventy
winters ;
Hearty and hale was he, an oak that is covered with
snow-flakes ;
White as the snow were his locks, and his cheeks as
brown as the oak-leaves.
Fair was she to behold, that maiden of seventeen sum-
mers.
Black were her eyes as the berry that grows on the thorn
by the wayside,
Black, yet how softly they gleamed beneath the brown
shade of her tresses !
Sweet was her breath as the breath of kine that feed in
the meadows.
When in the harvest heat she bore to the reapers at
noontide
Flagons of home-brewed ale, ah ! fair in sooth was the
maiden.
Fair was she when, on Sunday morn, while the bell
from its turret
Sprinkled with holy sounds the air, as the priest with
his hyssop
Sprinkles the congregation, and scatters blessings upon
them,

Homeward serenely she walked with God's benediction upon her.
When she had passed, it seemed like the ceasing of exquisite music

Down the long street she passed, with her chaplet of
    beads and her missal,
Wearing her Norman cap, and her kirtle of blue, and
    the ear-rings,
Brought in the olden time from France, and since, as
    an heirloom,
Handed down from mother to child, through long gen-
    erations.
But a celestial brightness — a more ethereal beauty —
Shone on her face and encircled her form, when, after
    confession,
Homeward serenely she walked with God's benediction
    upon her.
When she had passed, it seemed like the ceasing of
    exquisite music.

    Firmly builded with rafters of oak, the house of the
    farmer
Stood on the side of a hill commanding the sea ; and a
    shady
Sycamore grew by the door, with a woodbine wreathing
    around it.
Rudely carved was the porch, with seats beneath ; and
    a footpath
Led through an orchard wide, and disappeared in the
    meadow.
Under the sycamore-tree were hives overhung by a
    penthouse,

Such as the traveller sees in regions remote by the road-
side,
Built o'er a box for the poor, or the blessed image of
Mary.
Farther down, on the slope of the hill, was the well with
its moss-grown
Bucket, fastened with iron, and near it a trough for the
horses.
Shielding the house from storms, on the north, were the
barns and the farm-yard.
There stood the broad-wheeled wains and the antique
ploughs and the harrows ;
There were the folds for the sheep ; and there, in his
feathered seraglio,
Strutted the lordly turkey, and crowed the cock, with
the selfsame
Voice that in ages of old had startled the penitent Peter.
Bursting with hay were the barns, themselves a village.
In each one
Far o'er the gable projected a roof of thatch ; and a
staircase,
Under the sheltering eaves, led up to the odorous corn-
loft.
There too the dove-cot stood, with its meek and inno-
cent inmates
Murmuring ever of love ; while above in the variant
breezes
Numberless noisy weathercocks rattled and sang of
mutation.

Thus, at peace with God and the world, the farmer
of Grand-Pré
Lived on his sunny farm, and Evangeline governed his
household.
Many a youth, as he knelt in church and opened his
missal,
Fixed his eyes upon her as the saint of his deepest
devotion ;
Happy was he who might touch her hand or the hem
of her garment !
Many a suitor came to her door by the darkness be-
friended,
And, as he knocked and waited to hear the sound of her
footsteps,
Knew not which beat the louder, his heart or the
knocker of iron ;
Or at the joyous feast of the Patron Saint of the village,
Bolder grew, and pressed her hand in the dance as he
whispered
Hurried words of love, that seemed a part of the music.
But, among all who came, young Gabriel only was
welcome ;
Gabriel Lajeunesse, the son of Basil the blacksmith,
Who was a mighty man in the village, and honored of
all men ;
For, since the birth of time, throughout all ages and
nations
Has the craft of the smith been held in repute by the
people.

Basil was Benedict's friend. Their children from earliest childhood

Grew up together as brother and sister ; and Father Felician,

Priest and pedagogue both in the village, had taught them their letters

Out of the selfsame book, with the hymns of the church and the plain-song.

But when the hymn was sung, and the daily lesson completed,

Swiftly they hurried away to the forge of Basil the blacksmith.

There at the door they stood, with wondering eyes to behold him

Take in his leathern lap the hoof of the horse as a plaything,

Nailing the shoe in its place ; while near him the tire of the cart-wheel

Lay like a fiery snake, coiled round in a circle of cinders.

Oft on autumnal eves, when without in the gathering darkness

Bursting with light seemed the smithy, through every cranny and crevice,

Warm by the forge within they watched the laboring bellows,

And as its panting ceased, and the sparks expired in the ashes,

Merrily laughed, and said they were nuns going into
    the chapel.
Oft on sledges in winter, as swift as the swoop of the
    eagle,
Down the hillside bounding, they glided away o'er the
    meadow.
Oft in the barns they climbed to the populous nests on
    the rafters,
Seeking with eager eyes that wondrous stone, which
    the swallow
Brings from the shore of the sea to restore the sight of
    its fledglings ;
Lucky was he who found that stone in the nest of the
    swallow !
Thus passed a few swift years, and they no longer were
    children.
He was a valiant youth, and his face, like the face of
    the morning,
Gladdened the earth with its light, and ripened thought
    into action.
She was a woman now, with the heart and hopes of a
    woman.
" Sunshine of Saint Eulalie " was she called ; for that
    was the sunshine
Which, as the farmers believed, would load their or-
    chards with apples ;
She, too, would bring to her husband's house delight
    and abundance,
Filling it with love and the ruddy faces of children.

II

Now had the season returned, when the nights grow
  colder and longer,
And the retreating sun the sign of the Scorpion enters.
Birds of passage sailed through the leaden air, from the
  ice-bound,
Desolate northern bays to the shores of tropical islands.
Harvests were gathered in ; and wild with the winds of
  September
Wrestled the trees of the forest, as Jacob of old with the
  angel.
All the signs foretold a winter long and inclement.
Bees, with prophetic instinct of want, had hoarded their
  honey
Till the hives overflowed ; and the Indian hunters as-
  serted
Cold would the winter be, for thick was the fur of the
  foxes.
Such was the advent of autumn. Then followed that
  beautiful season,
Called by the pious Acadian peasants the Summer of
  All-Saints !
Filled was the air with a dreamy and magical light ; and
  the landscape
Lay as if new-created in all the freshness of childhood.
Peace seemed to reign upon earth, and the restless heart
  of the ocean
Was for a moment consoled. All sounds were in har-
  mony blended.

Voices of children at play, the crowing of cocks in the
farm-yards,
Whir of wings in the drowsy air, and the cooing of
pigeons,
All were subdued and low as the murmurs of love, and
the great sun
Looked with the eye of love through the golden vapors
around him ;
While arrayed in its robes of russet and scarlet and
yellow,
Bright with the sheen of the dew, each glittering tree
of the forest
Flashed like the plane-tree the Persian adorned with
mantles and jewels.

Now recommenced the reign of rest and affection and
stillness.
Day with its burden and heat had departed, and twi-
light descending
Brought back the evening star to the sky, and the herds
to the homestead.
Pawing the ground they came, and resting their necks
on each other,
And with their nostrils distended inhaling the freshness
of evening.
Foremost, bearing the bell, Evangeline's beautiful
heifer,
Proud of her snow-white hide, and the ribbon that
waved from her collar,

Quietly paced and slow, as if conscious of human affection.

Then came the shepherd back with his bleating flocks from the seaside,

Where was their favorite pasture. Behind them followed the watch-dog,

Patient, full of importance, and grand in the pride of his instinct,

Walking from side to side with a lordly air, and superbly

Waving his bushy tail, and urging forward the stragglers;

Regent of flocks was he when the shepherd slept; their protector,

When from the forest at night, through the starry silence the wolves howled.

Late, with the rising moon, returned the wains from the marshes,

Laden with briny hay, that filled the air with its odor.

Cheerily neighed the steeds, with dew on their manes and their fetlocks,

While aloft on their shoulders the wooden and ponderous saddles,

Painted with brilliant dyes, and adorned with tassels of crimson,

Nodded in bright array, like hollyhocks heavy with blossoms.

Patiently stood the cows meanwhile, and yielded their udders

Unto the milkmaid's hand ; whilst loud and in regular
cadence
Into the sounding pails the foaming streamlets de-
scended.
Lowing of cattle and peals of laughter were heard in the
farm-yard,
Echoed back by the barns. Anon they sank into still-
ness ;
Heavily closed, with a jarring sound, the valves of the
barn-doors,
Rattled the wooden bars, and all for a season was
silent.

In-doors, warm by the wide-mouthed fireplace, idly
the farmer
Sat in his elbow-chair and watched how the flames and
the smoke-wreaths
Struggled together like foes in a burning city. Behind
him,
Nodding and mocking along the wall, with gestures
fantastic,
Darted his own huge shadow, and vanished away into
darkness.
Faces, clumsily carved in oak, on the back of his arm-
chair
Laughed in the flickering light ; and the pewter plates
on the dresser
Caught and reflected the flame, as shields of armies the
sunshine.

Fragments of song the old man sang, and carols of
    Christmas,
Such as at home, in the olden time, his fathers before
    him
Sang in their Norman orchards and bright Burgundian
    vineyards.
Close at her father's side was the gentle Evangeline
    seated,
Spinning flax for the loom, that stood in the corner
    behind her.
Silent awhile were its treadles, at rest was its diligent
    shuttle,
While the monotonous drone of the wheel, like the
    drone of a bagpipe,
Followed the old man's song and united the fragments
    together.
As in a church, when the chant of the choir at intervals
    ceases,
Footfalls are heard in the aisles, or words of the priest
    at the altar,
So, in each pause of the song, with measured motion
    the clock clicked.

Thus as they sat, there were footsteps heard, and
    suddenly lifted,
Sounded the wooden latch, and the door swung back
    on its hinges.
Benedict knew by the hob-nailed shoes it was Basil the
    blacksmith,

And by her beating heart Evangeline knew who was
with him.

"Welcome ! " the farmer exclaimed, as their footsteps
paused on the threshold,

"Welcome, Basil, my friend ! Come, take thy place on
the settle

Close by the chimney-side, which is always empty
without thee ;

Take from the shelf overhead thy pipe and the box of
tobacco ;

Never so much thyself art thou as when through the
curling

Smoke of the pipe or the forge thy friendly and jovial
face gleams

Round and red as the harvest moon through the mist of
the marshes."

Then, with a smile of content, thus answered Basil the
blacksmith,

Taking with easy air the accustomed seat by the fire-
side : —

" Benedict Bellefontaine, thou hast ever thy jest and
thy ballad !

Ever in cheerfullest mood art thou, when others are
filled with

Gloomy forebodings of ill and see only ruin before
them.

Happy art thou, as if every day thou hadst picked up a
horseshoe."

Pausing a moment, to take the pipe that Evangeline
brought him,
And with a coal from the embers had lighted, he slowly
continued : —
" Four days now are passed since the English ships at
their anchors
Ride in the Gaspereau's mouth, with their cannon
pointed against us.
What their design may be is unknown ; but all are
commanded
On the morrow to meet in the church, where his
Majesty's mandate
Will be proclaimed as law in the land. Alas ! in the
mean time
Many surmises of evil alarm the hearts of the peo-
ple."
Then made answer the farmer : " Perhaps some friend-
lier purpose
Brings these ships to our shores. Perhaps the harvests
in England
By untimely rains or untimelier heat have been blighted,
And from our bursting barns they would feed their
cattle and children."
" Not so thinketh the folk in the village," said, warmly,
the blacksmith,
Shaking his head, as in doubt ; then, heaving a sigh,
he continued : —
" Louisburg is not forgotten, nor Beau Séjour, nor
Port Royal.

Many already have fled to the forest, and lurk on its
    outskirts,
Waiting with anxious hearts the dubious fate of to-
    morrow.
Arms have been taken from us, and warlike weapons
    of all kinds ;
Nothing is left but the blacksmith's sledge and the
    scythe of the mower."
Then with a pleasant smile made answer the jovial
    farmer : —
" Safer are we unarmed, in the midst of our flocks and
    our cornfields,
Safer within these peaceful dikes, besieged by the ocean,
Than our fathers in forts, besieged by the enemy's
    cannon.
Fear no evil, my friend, and to-night may no shadow of
    sorrow
Fall on this house and hearth ; for this is the night of
    the contract.
Built are the house and the barn. The merry lads of the
    village
Strongly have built them and well ; and, breaking the
    glebe round about them,
Filled the barn with hay, and the house with food for a
    twelvemonth.
René Leblanc will be here anon, with his papers and
    inkhorn.
Shall we not then be glad, and rejoice in the joy of our
    children ? "

As apart by the window she stood, with her hand in her
lover's,
Blushing Evangeline heard the words that her father
had spoken,
And, as they died on his lips, the worthy notary entered.

III

Bent like a laboring oar, that toils in the surf of the
ocean,
Bent, but not broken, by age was the form of the notary
public ;
Shocks of yellow hair, like the silken floss of the maize,
hung
Over his shoulders ; his forehead was high ; and
glasses with horn bows
Sat astride on his nose, with a look of wisdom super-
nal.
Father of twenty children was he, and more than a
hundred
Children's children rode on his knee, and heard his
great watch tick.
Four long years in the times of the war had he lan-
guished a captive,
Suffering much in an old French fort as the friend of
the English.
Now, though warier grown, without all guile or sus-
picion,
Ripe in wisdom was he, but patient, and simple, and
childlike.

He was beloved by all, and most of all by the children ;

For he told them tales of the Loup-garou in the forest,

And of the goblin that came in the night to water the horses,

And of the white Létiche, the ghost of a child who un-christened

Died, and was doomed to haunt unseen the chambers of children ;

And how on Christmas eve the oxen talked in the stable,

And how the fever was cured by a spider shut up in a nutshell,

And of the marvellous powers of four-leaved clover and horseshoes,

With whatsoever else was writ in the lore of the vil-lage.

Then up rose from his seat by the fireside Basil the blacksmith,

Knocked from his pipe the ashes, and slowly extending his right hand,

" Father Leblanc," he exclaimed, " thou hast heard the talk in the village,

And, perchance, canst tell us some news of these ships and their errand."

Then with modest demeanor made answer the notary public, —

" Gossip enough have I heard, in sooth, yet am never the wiser ;

And what their errand may be I know not better than others.

Yet am I not of those who imagine some evil intention
Brings them here, for we are at peace ; and why then
    molest us ? ''
''God's name!'' shouted the hasty and somewhat iras-
    cible blacksmith ;
'' Must we in all things look for the how, and the why,
    and the wherefore ?
Daily injustice is done, and might is the right of the
    strongest ! ''
But without heeding his warmth, continued the notary
    public, —
'' Man is unjust, but God is just ; and finally justice
Triumphs ; and well I remember a story, that often
    consoled me,
When as a captive I lay in the old French fort at Port
    Royal.''
This was the old man's favorite tale, and he loved to
    repeat it
When his neighbors complained that any injustice was
    done them.
'' Once in an ancient city, whose name I no longer
    remember,
Raised aloft on a column, a brazen statue of Justice
Stood in the public square, upholding the scales in its
    left hand,
And in its right a sword, as an emblem that justice pre-
    sided
Over the laws of the land, and the hearts and homes of
    the people.

Even the birds had built their nests in the scales of the
balance,
Having no fear of the sword that flashed in the sunshine
above them.
But in the course of time the laws of the land were
corrupted ;
Might took the place of right, and the weak were op-
pressed, and the mighty
Ruled with an iron rod. Then it chanced in a noble-
man's palace
That a necklace of pearls was lost, and erelong a sus-
picion
Fell on an orphan girl who lived as a maid in the
household.
She, after form of trial condemned to die on the scaf-
fold,
Patiently met her doom at the foot of the statue of
Justice.
As to her Father in heaven her innocent spirit ascended,
Lo ! o'er the city a tempest rose ; and the bolts of the
thunder
Smote the statue of bronze, and hurled in wrath from its
left hand
Down on the pavement below the clattering scales of the
balance,
And in the hollow thereof was found the nest of a
magpie,
Into whose clay-built walls the necklace of pearls was
inwoven."

Silenced, but not convinced, when the story was ended, the blacksmith
Stood like a man who fain would speak, but findeth no language ;
All his thoughts were congealed into lines on his face, as the vapors
Freeze in fantastic shapes on the window-panes in the winter.

Then Evangeline lighted the brazen lamp on the table,
Filled, till it overflowed, the pewter tankard with home-brewed
Nut-brown ale, that was famed for its strength in the village of Grand-Pré ;
While from his pocket the notary drew his papers and inkhorn,
Wrote with a steady hand the date and the age of the parties,
Naming the dower of the bride in flocks of sheep and in cattle.
Orderly all things proceeded, and duly and well were completed,
And the great seal of the law was set like a sun on the margin.
Then from his leathern pouch the farmer threw on the table
Three times the old man's fee in solid pieces of silver ;
And the notary rising, and blessing the bride and the bridegroom,

Lifted aloft the tankard of ale and drank to their wel-
fare.

Wiping the foam from his lip, he solemnly bowed and
departed,

While in silence the others sat and mused by the fire-
side,

Till Evangeline brought the draught-board out of its
corner.

Soon was the game begun. In friendly contention the
old men

Laughed at each lucky hit, or unsuccessful manœuvre,

Laughed when a man was crowned, or a breach was
made in the king-row.

Meanwhile apart, in the twilight gloom of a window's
embrasure,

Sat the lovers, and whispered together, beholding the
moon rise

Over the pallid sea, and the silvery mists of the
meadows.

Silently one by one, in the infinite meadows of heaven,

Blossomed the lovely stars, the forget-me-nots of the
angels.

Thus was the evening passed. Anon the bell from
the belfry

Rang out the hour of nine, the village curfew, and
straightway

Rose the guests and departed; and silence reigned in
the household.

Many a farewell word and sweet good-night on the
   door-step
Lingered long in Evangeline's heart, and filled it with
   gladness.
Carefully then were covered the embers that glowed on
   the hearth-stone,
And on the oaken stairs resounded the tread of the
   farmer.
Soon with a soundless step the foot of Evangeline fol-
   lowed.
Up the staircase moved a luminous space in the dark-
   ness,
Lighted less by the lamp than the shining face of the
   maiden.
Silent she passed the hall, and entered the door of her
   chamber.
Simple that chamber was, with its curtains of white
   and its clothes-press
Ample and high, on whose spacious shelves were care-
   fully folded
Linen and woollen stuffs, by the hand of Evangeline
   woven.
This was the precious dower she would bring to her
   husband in marriage,
Better than flocks and herds, being proofs of her skill
   as a housewife.
Soon she extinguished her lamp, for the mellow and
   radiant moonlight

Streamed through the windows, and lighted the room
    till the heart of the maiden
Swelled and obeyed its power, like the tremulous tides
    of the ocean.
Ah! she was fair, exceeding fair to behold, as she stood
    with
Naked snow-white feet on the gleaming floor of her
    chamber!
Little she dreamed that below, among the trees of the
    orchard,
Waited her lover and watched for the gleam of her lamp
    and her shadow.
Yet were her thoughts of him, and at times a feeling of
    sadness
Passed o'er her soul, as the sailing shade of clouds in
    the moonlight
Flitted across the floor and darkened the room for a
    moment.
And, as she gazed from the window, she saw serenely
    the moon pass
Forth from the folds of a cloud, and one star follow her
    footsteps,
As out of Abraham's tent young Ishmael wandered with
    Hagar!

IV

Pleasantly rose next morn the sun on the village of
    Grand-Pré.
Pleasantly gleamed in the soft, sweet air the Basin of
    Minas,

Where the ships, with their wavering shadows, were
riding at anchor.
Life had long been astir in the village, and clamorous
labor
Knocked with its hundred hands at the golden gates of
the morning.
Now from the country around, from the farms and
neighboring hamlets,
Came in their holiday dresses the blithe Acadian peas-
ants.
Many a glad good-morrow and jocund laugh from the
young folk
Made the bright air brighter, as up from the numerous
meadows,
Where no path could be seen but the track of wheels in
the greensward,
Group after group appeared, and joined, or passed on
the highway.
Long ere noon, in the village all sounds of labor were
silenced.
Thronged were the streets with people; and noisy
groups at the house-doors
Sat in the cheerful sun, and rejoiced and gossiped to-
gether.
Every house was an inn, where all were welcomed and
feasted;
For with this simple people, who lived like brothers to-
gether,

All things were held in common, and what one had was
  another's.
Yet under Benedict's roof hospitality seemed more
  abundant:
For Evangeline stood among the guests of her father;
Bright was her face with smiles, and words of welcome
  and gladness
Fell from her beautiful lips, and blessed the cup as she
  gave it.

Under the open sky, in the odorous air of the orchard,
Stript of its golden fruit, was spread the feast of be-
  trothal.
There in the shade of the porch were the priest and the
  notary seated;
There good Benedict sat, and sturdy Basil the black-
  smith.
Not far withdrawn from these, by the cider-press and
  the beehives,
Michael the fiddler was placed, with the gayest of hearts
  and of waistcoats.
Shadow and light from the leaves alternately played on
  his snow-white
Hair, as it waved in the wind; and the jolly face of the
  fiddler
Glowed like a living coal when the ashes are blown
  from the embers.
Gayly the old man sang to the vibrant sound of his
  fiddle,

Tous les Bourgeois de Chartres, and *Le Carillon de Dun-
quevque,*
And anon with his wooden shoes beat time to the music.
Merrily, merrily whirled the wheels of the dizzying
dances
Under the orchard-trees and down the path to the
meadows;
Old folk and young together, and children mingled
among them.
Fairest of all the maids was Evangeline, Benedict's
daughter!
Noblest of all the youths was Gabriel, son of the black-
smith!

So passed the morning away. And lo! with a sum-
mons sonorous
Sounded the bell from its tower, and over the meadows
a drum beat.
Thronged erelong was the church with men. Without,
in the churchyard,
Waited the women. They stood by the graves, and
hung on the headstones
Garlands of autumn-leaves and evergreens fresh from
the forest.
Then came the guard from the ships, and marching
proudly among them
Entered the sacred portal. With loud and dissonant
clangor

Echoed the sound of their brazen drums from ceiling
and casement, —
Echoed a moment only, and slowly the ponderous
portal
Closed, and in silence the crowd awaited the will of the
soldiers.
Then uprose their commander, and spake from the
steps of the altar,
Holding aloft in his hands, with its seals, the royal
commission.
" You are convened this day," he said, " by his Ma-
jesty's orders.
Clement and kind has he been; but how you have
answered his kindness,
Let your own hearts reply ! To my natural make and
my temper
Painful the task is I do, which to you I know must be
grievous.
Yet must I bow and obey, and deliver the will of our
monarch ;
Namely, that all your lands, and dwellings, and cattle
of all kinds
Forfeited be to the crown ; and that you yourselves from
this province
Be transported to other lands. God grant you may dwell
there
Ever as faithful subjects, a happy and peaceable people !
Prisoners now I declare you ; for such is his Majesty's
pleasure ! "

As, when the air is serene in sultry solstice of summer,
Suddenly gathers a storm, and the deadly sling of the
hailstones
Beats down the farmer's corn in the field and shatters
his windows,
Hiding the sun, and strewing the ground with thatch
from the house-roofs,
Bellowing fly the herds, and seek to break their enclo-
sures ;
So on the hearts of the people descended the words of
the speaker.
Silent a moment they stood in speechless wonder, and
then rose
Louder and ever louder a wail of sorrow and anger,
And, by one impulse moved, they madly rushed to the
door-way.
Vain was the hope of escape ; and cries and fierce im-
precations
Rang through the house of prayer ; and high o'er the
heads of the others
Rose, with his arms uplifted, the figure of Basil the
blacksmith,
As, on a stormy sea, a spar is tossed by the billows.
Flushed was his face and distorted with passion ; and
wildly he shouted, —
"Down with the tyrants of England ! we never have
sworn them allegiance !
Death to these foreign soldiers, who seize on our homes
and our harvests ! "

More he fain would have said, but the merciless hand
    of a soldier
Smote him upon the mouth, and dragged him down to
    the pavement.

In the midst of the strife and tumult of angry con-
    tention,
Lo! the door of the chancel opened, and Father Felician
Entered, with serious mien, and ascended the steps of
    the altar.
Raising his reverend hand, with a gesture he awed into
    silence
All that clamorous throng ; and thus he spake to his
    people ;
Deep were his tones and solemn ; in accents measured
    and mournful
Spake he, as, after the tocsin's alarum, distinctly the
    clock strikes.
" What is this that ye do, my children? what madness
    has seized you?
Forty years of my life have I labored among you, and
    taught you,
Not in word alone, but in deed, to love one another !
Is this the fruit of my toils, of my vigils and prayers
    and privations?
Have you so soon forgotten all lessons of love and for-
    giveness?
This is the house of the Prince of Peace, and would you
    profane it

Thus with violent deeds and hearts overflowing with
    hatred?
Lo ! where the crucified Christ from his cross is gazing
    upon you !
See ! in those sorrowful eyes what meekness and holy
    compassion !
Hark ! how those lips still repeat the prayer, ' O Father,
    forgive them ! '
Let us repeat that prayer in the hour when the wicked
    assail us,
Let us repeat it now, and say, ' O Father, forgive
    them ! ' ''
Few were his words of rebuke, but deep in the hearts of
    his people
Sank they, and sobs of contrition succeeded the pas-
    sionate outbreak,
While they repeated his prayer, and said, '' O Father,
    forgive them ! ''

Then came the evening service. The tapers gleamed
    from the altar.
Fervent and deep was the voice of the priest, and the
    people responded,
Not with their lips alone, but their hearts ; and the Ave
    Maria
Sang they, and fell on their knees, and their souls, with
    devotion translated,
Rose on the ardor of prayer, like Elijah ascending to
    heaven.

Meanwhile had spread in the village the tidings of
ill, and on all sides
Wandered, wailing, from house to house the women
and children.
Long at her father's door Evangeline stood, with her
right hand
Shielding her eyes from the level rays of the sun, that,
descending,
Lighted the village street with mysterious splendor, and
roofed each
Peasant's cottage with golden thatch, and emblazoned
its windows.
Long within had been spread the snow-white cloth on
the table ;
There stood the wheaten loaf, and the honey fragrant
with wild-flowers ;
There stood the tankard of ale, and the cheese fresh
brought from the dairy,
And, at the head of the board, the great arm-chair of
the farmer.
Thus did Evangeline wait at her father's door, as the
sunset
Threw the long shadows of trees o'er the broad ambro-
sial meadows.
Ah ! on her spirit within a deeper shadow had fallen,
And from the fields of her soul a fragrance celestial
ascended, —
Charity, meekness, love, and hope, and forgiveness,
and patience !

Then, all-forgetful of self, she wandered into the village,

Cheering with looks and words the mournful hearts of the women,

As o'er the darkening fields with lingering steps they departed,

Urged by their household cares, and the weary feet of their children.

Down sank the great red sun, and in golden, glimmering vapors

Veiled the light of his face, like the Prophet descending from Sinai.

Sweetly over the village the bell of the Angelus sounded.

Meanwhile, amid the gloom, by the church Evangeline lingered.

All was silent within ; and in vain at the door and the windows

Stood she, and listened and looked, till, overcome by emotion

"Gabriel!" cried she aloud with tremulous voice ; but no answer

Came from the graves of the dead, nor the gloomier grave of the living.

Slowly at length she returned to the tenantless house of her father.

Smouldered the fire on the hearth, on the board was the supper untasted,

Empty and drear was each room, and haunted with phantoms of terror.

Sadly echoed her step on the stair and the floor of her
chamber.

In the dead of the night she heard the disconsolate rain
fall

Loud on the withered leaves of the sycamore-tree by
the window.

Keenly the lightning flashed ; and the voice of the echo-
ing thunder

Told her that God was in heaven, and governed the
world he created !

Then she remembered the tale she had heard of the
justice of Heaven ;

Soothed was her troubled soul, and she peacefully slum-
bered till morning.

ˇ

Four times the sun had risen and set ; and now on the
fifth day

Cheerily called the cock to the sleeping maids of the
farm-house.

Soon o'er the yellow fields, in silent and mournful pro-
cession,

Came from the neighboring hamlets and farms the Aca-
dian women,

Driving in ponderous wains their household goods to
the sea-shore,

Pausing and looking back to gaze once more on their
dwellings,

Ere they were shut from sight by the winding road and
the woodland.

Close at their sides their children ran, and urged on the
oxen,

While in their little hands they clasped some fragments
of playthings.

Thus to the Gaspereau's mouth they hurried ; and
there on the sea-beach

Piled in confusion lay the household goods of the
peasants.

All day long between the shore and the ships did the
boats ply ;

All day long the wains came laboring down from the
village.

Late in the afternoon, when the sun was near to his
setting,

Echoed far o'er the fields came the roll of drums from
the churchyard.

Thither the women and children thronged. On a sud-
den the church-doors

Opened, and forth came the guard, and marching in
gloomy procession

Followed the long-imprisoned, but patient, Acadian
farmers.

Even as pilgrims, who journey afar from their homes
and their country,

Sing as they go, and in singing forget they are weary
and wayworn,

So with songs on their lips the Acadian peasants de-
scended

Down from the church to the shore, amid their wives
and their daughters.

Foremost the young men came ; and, raising together
their voices,

Sang with tremulous lips a chant of the Catholic Mis-
sions : —

"Sacred heart of the Saviour ! O inexhaustible foun-
tain !

Fill our hearts this day with strength and submission
and patience ! ''

Then the old men, as they marched, and the women
that stood by the wayside

Joined in the sacred psalm, and the birds in the sun-
shine above them

Mingled their notes therewith, like voices of spirits de-
parted.

Half-way down to the shore Evangeline waited in
silence,

Not overcome with grief, but strong in the hour of
affliction, —

Calmly and sadly she waited, until the procession ap-
proached her,

And she beheld the face of Gabriel pale with emo-
tion.

Tears then filled her eyes, and, eagerly running to meet
him,

Clasped she his hands, and laid her head on his shoul-
    der, and whispered, —
" Gabriel ! be of good cheer ! for if we love one an-
    other
Nothing, in truth, can harm us, whatever mischances
    may happen ! "
Smiling she spake these words ; then suddenly paused,
    for her father
Saw she slowly advancing. Alas ! how changed was
    his aspect !
Gone was the glow from his cheek, and the fire from his
    eye, and his footstep
Heavier seemed with the weight of the heavy heart in
    his bosom.
But with a smile and a sigh, she clasped his neck and
    embraced him,
Speaking words of endearment where words of comfort
    availed not.
Thus to the Gaspereau's mouth moved on that mourn-
    ful procession.

There disorder prevailed, and the tumult and stir of
    embarking.
Busily plied the freighted boats ; and in the confusion
Wives were torn from their husbands, and mothers, too
    late, saw their children
Left on the land, extending their arms, with wildest
    entreaties.
So unto separate ships were Basil and Gabriel carried,

While in despair on the shore Evangeline stood with
    her father.

Half the task was not done when the sun went down,
    and the twilight

Deepened and darkened around ; and in haste the
    refluent ocean

Fled away from the shore, and left the line of the sand-
    beach

Covered with waifs of the tide, with kelp and the slip-
    pery sea-weed.

Farther back in the midst of the household goods and
    the wagons,

Like to a gypsy camp, or a leaguer after a battle,

All escape cut off by the sea, and the sentinels near
    them,

Lay encamped for the night the houseless Acadian
    farmers.

Back to its nethermost caves retreated the bellowing
    ocean,

Dragging adown the beach the rattling pebbles, and
    leaving

Inland and far up the shore the stranded boats of the
    sailors.

Then, as the night descended, the herds returned from
    their pastures ;

Sweet was the moist still air with the odor of milk from
    their udders ;

Lowing they waited, and long, at the well-known bars
    of the farm-yard, —

Waited and looked in vain for the voice and the hand
of the milk-maid.
Silence reigned in the streets; from the church no
Angelus sounded,
Rose no smoke from the roofs, and gleamed no lights
from the windows.

But on the shores meanwhile the evening fires had
been kindled,
Built of the drift-wood thrown on the sands from wrecks
in the tempest.
Round them shapes of gloom and sorrowful faces were
gathered,
Voices of women were heard, and of men, and the
crying of children.
Onward from fire to fire, as from hearth to hearth in his
parish,
Wandered the faithful priest, consoling and blessing
and cheering,
Like unto shipwrecked Paul on Melita's desolate sea-
shore.
Thus he approached the place where Evangeline sat
with her father,
And in the flickering light beheld the face of the old
man,
Haggard and hollow and wan, and without either
thought or emotion,
E'en as the face of a clock from which the hands have
been taken.

Vainly Evangeline strove with words and caresses to
    cheer him,
Vainly offered him food ; yet he moved not, he looked
    not, he spake not,
But, with a vacant stare, ever gazed at the flickering
    fire-light.
"*Benedicite!*" murmured the priest, in tones of com-
    passion.
More he fain would have said, but his heart was full,
    and his accents
Faltered and paused on his lips, as the feet of a child on
    a threshold,
Hushed by the scene he beholds, and the awful pre-
    sence of sorrow.
Silently, therefore, he laid his hand on the head of the
    maiden,
Raising his tearful eyes to the silent stars that above
    them
Moved on their way, unperturbed by the wrongs and
    sorrows of mortals.
Then sat he down at her side, and they wept together
    in silence.

Suddenly rose from the south a light, as in autumn
    the blood-red
Moon climbs the crystal walls of heaven, and o'er the
    horizon
Titan-like stretches its hundred hands upon mountain
    and meadow,

Seizing the rocks and the rivers and piling huge
    shadows together.
Broader and ever broader it gleamed on the roofs of the
    village,
Gleamed on the sky and sea, and the ships that lay in
    the roadstead.
Columns of shining smoke uprose, and flashes of flame
    were
Thrust through their folds and withdrawn, like the
    quivering hands of a martyr.
Then as the wind seized the gleeds and the burning
    thatch, and, uplifting,
Whirled them aloft through the air, at once from a
    hundred house-tops
Started the sheeted smoke with flashes of flame inter-
    mingled.

These things beheld in dismay the crowd on the
    shore and on shipboard.
Speechless at first they stood, then cried aloud in their
    anguish,
"We shall behold no more our homes in the village of
    Grand-Pré!"
Loud on a sudden the cocks began to crow in the farm-
    yards,
Thinking the day had dawned; and anon the lowing
    of cattle
Came on the evening breeze, by the barking of dogs
    interrupted.

Then rose a sound of dread, such as startles the sleep-
ing encampments

Far in the western prairies or forests that skirt the
Nebraska,

When the wild horses affrighted sweep by with the
speed of the whirlwind,

Or the loud bellowing herds of buffaloes rush to the
river.

Such was the sound that arose on the night, as the
herds and the horses

Broke through their folds and fences, and madly rushed
o'er the meadows.

Overwhelmed with the sight, yet speechless, the
priest and the maiden

Gazed on the scene of terror that reddened and widened
before them ;

And as they turned at length to speak to their silent
companion,

Lo! from his seat he had fallen, and stretched abroad
on the sea-shore

Motionless lay his form, from which the soul had de-
parted.

Slowly the priest uplifted the lifeless head, and the
maiden

Knelt at her father's side, and wailed aloud in her ter-
ror.

Then in a swoon she sank, and lay with her head on his
bosom.

Through the long night she lay in deep, oblivious
  slumber;
And when she awoke from the trance, she beheld a
  multitude near her.
Faces of friends she beheld, that were mournfully gaz-
  ing upon her,
Pallid, with tearful eyes, and looks of saddest com-
  passion.
Still the blaze of the burning village illumined the land-
  scape,
Reddened the sky overhead, and gleamed on the faces
  around her,
And like the day of doom it seemed to her wavering
  senses.
Then a familiar voice she heard, as it said to the
  people, —
"Let us bury him here by the sea. When a happier
  season
Brings us again to our homes from the unknown land
  of our exile,
Then shall his sacred dust be piously laid in the church-
  yard."
Such were the words of the priest. And there in haste
  by the sea-side,
Having the glare of the burning village for funeral
  torches,
But without bell or book, they buried the farmer of
  Grand-Pré.

And as the voice of the priest repeated the service of
sorrow,

Lo ! with a mournful sound, like the voice of a vast
congregation,

Solemnly answered the sea, and mingled its roar with
the dirges.

'T was the returning tide, that afar from the waste of
the ocean,

With the first dawn of the day, came heaving and
hurrying landward.

Then recommenced once more the stir and noise of
embarking ;

And with the ebb of the tide the ships sailed out of the
harbor,

Leaving behind them the dead on the shore, and the
village in ruins.

THE SONG OF HIAWATHA

HIAWATHA'S SAILING

"Give me of your bark, O Birch-tree !
Of your yellow bark, O Birch-tree !
Growing by the rushing river,
Tall and stately in the valley !
I a light canoe will build me,
Build a swift Cheemaun for sailing,
That shall float upon the river,
Like a yellow leaf in Autumn,
Like a yellow water-lily !
   " Lay aside your cloak, O Birch-tree !
Lay aside your white-skin wrapper,
For the Summer-time is coming,
And the sun is warm in heaven,
And you need no white-skin wrapper ! "
   Thus aloud cried Hiawatha
In the solitary forest,
By the rushing Taquamenaw,
When the birds were singing gayly,
In the Moon of Leaves were singing,
And the sun, from sleep awaking,
Started up and said, " Behold me !
Geezis, the great Sun, behold me ! "
   And the tree with all its branches
Rustled in the breeze of morning,

Saying, with a sigh of patience,
" Take my cloak, O Hiawatha ! "
   With his knife the tree he girdled ;
Just beneath its lowest branches,
Just above the roots, he cut it,
Till the sap came oozing outward ;
Down the trunk, from top to bottom,
Sheer he cleft the bark asunder,
With a wooden wedge he raised it,
Stripped it from the trunk unbroken.
   " Give me of your boughs, O Cedar !
Of your strong and pliant branches,
My canoe to make more steady,
Make more strong and firm beneath me ! "
   Through the summit of the Cedar
Went a sound, a cry of horror,
Went a murmur of resistance ;
But it whispered, bending downward,
" Take my boughs, O Hiawatha ! "
   Down he hewed the boughs of cedar,
Shaped them straightway to a frame-work,
Like two bows he formed and shaped them,
Like two bended bows together.
   " Give me of your roots, O Tamarack !
Of your fibrous roots, O Larch-tree !
My canoe to bind together,
So to bind the ends together
That the water may not enter,
That the river may not wet me ! "

And the Larch, with all its fibres,
Shivered in the air of morning,
Touched his forehead with its tassels,
Said, with one long sigh of sorrow,
" Take them all, O Hiawatha ! "
    From the earth he tore the fibres,
Tore the tough roots of the Larch-tree,
Closely sewed the bark together,
Bound it closely to the frame-work.
    " Give me of your balm, O Fir-tree !
Of your balsam and your resin,
So to close the seams together
That the water may not enter,
That the river may not wet me ! "
    And the Fir-tree, tall and sombre,
Sobbed through all its robes of darkness,
Rattled like a shore with pebbles,
Answered wailing, answered weeping,
" Take my balm, O Hiawatha ! "
    And he took the tears of balsam,
Took the resin of the Fir-tree,
Smeared therewith each seam and fissure,
Made each crevice safe from water.
    " Give me of your quills, O Hedgehog !
All your quills, O Kagh, the Hedgehog !
I will make a necklace of them,
Make a girdle for my beauty,
And two stars to deck her bosom ! "
    From a hollow tree the Hedgehog

With his sleepy eyes looked at him,
Shot his shining quills, like arrows,
Saying with a drowsy murmur,
Through the tangle of his whiskers,
" Take my quills, O Hiawatha ! "
    From the ground the quills he gathered
All the little shining arrows,
Stained them red and blue and yellow,
With the juice of roots and berries ;
Into his canoe he wrought them,
Round its waist a shining girdle,
Round its bows a gleaming necklace,
On its breast two stars resplendent.
    Thus the Birch Canoe was builded
In the valley, by the river,
In the bosom of the forest ;
And the forest's life was in it,
All its mystery and its magic,
All the lightness of the birch-tree,
All the toughness of the cedar,
All the larch's supple sinews ;
And it floated on the river
Like a yellow leaf in Autumn,
Like a yellow water-lily.
    Paddles none had Hiawatha,
Paddles none he had or needed,
For his thoughts as paddles served him,
And his wishes served to guide him ;
Swift or slow at will he glided,

Veered to right or left at pleasure.

Then he called aloud to Kwasind,
To his friend, the strong man, Kwasind,
Saying, "Help me clear this river
Of its sunken logs and sand-bars."

Straight into the river Kwasind
Plunged as if he were an otter,
Dived as if he were a beaver,
Stood up to his waist in water,
To his arm-pits in the river,
Swam and shouted in the river,
Tugged at sunken logs and branches,
With his hands he scooped the sand-bars,
With his feet the ooze and tangle.

And thus sailed my Hiawatha
Down the rushing Taquamenaw,
Sailed through all its bends and windings,
Sailed through all its deeps and shallows
While his friend, the strong man, Kwasind,
Swam the deeps, the shallows waded.

Up and down the river went they,
In and out among its islands,
Cleared its bed of root and sand-bar,
Dragged the dead trees from its channel,
Made its passage safe and certain,
Made a pathway for the people,
From its springs among the mountains,
To the waters of Pauwating,
To the bay of Taquamenau.

HIAWATHA'S FISHING

FORTH upon the Gitchie Gumee,
On the shining Big-Sea-Water,
With his fishing-line of cedar,
Of the twisted bark of cedar,
Forth to catch the sturgeon Nahma,
Mishe-Nahma, King of Fishes,
In his birch canoe exulting
All alone went Hiawatha.
　　Through the clear, transparent water
He could see the fishes swimming
Far down in the depths below him;
See the yellow perch, the Sahwa,
Like a sunbeam in the water,
See the Shawgashee, the craw-fish,
Like a spider on the bottom,
On the white and sandy bottom.
　　At the stern sat Hiawatha,
With his fishing-line of cedar;
In his plumes the breeze of morning
Played as in the hemlock branches;
On the bows, with tail erected,
Sat the squirrel, Adjidaumo;
In his fur the breeze of morning
Played as in the prairie grasses.

135

On the white sand of the bottom
Lay the monster Mishe-Nahma,
Lay the sturgeon, King of Fishes;
Through his gills he breathed the water,
With his fins he fanned and winnowed,
With his tail he swept the sand-floor.
There he lay in all his armor;
On each side a shield to guard him,
Plates of bone upon his forehead,
Down his sides and back and shoulders
Plates of bone with spines projecting!
Painted was he with his war-paints
Stripes of yellow, red, and azure.
Spots of brown and spots of sable;
And he lay there on the bottom,
Fanning with his fins of purple,
As above him Hiawatha
In his birch canoe came sailing,
With his fishing-line of cedar.
"Take my bait," cried Hiawatha,
Down into the depths beneath him,
"Take my bait, O Sturgeon, Nahma!
Come up from below the water,
Let us see which is the stronger!"
And he dropped his line of cedar
Through the clear, transparent water,
Waited vainly for an answer,
Long sat waiting for an answer,
And repeating loud and louder,

And he dropped his line of cedar
Through the clear, transparent water

"Take my bait, O King of Fishes!"
    Quiet lay the sturgeon, Nahma,
  Fanning slowly in the water,
  Looking up at Hiawatha,
  Listening to his call and clamor,
  His unnecessary tumult,
  Till he wearied of the shouting;
  And he said to the Kenozha,
  To the pike, the Maskenozha,
"Take the bait of this rude fellow,
  Break the line of Hiawatha!"
    In his fingers Hiawatha
  Felt the loose line jerk and tighten;
  As he drew it in, it tugged so
  That the birch canoe stood endwise,
  Like a birch log in the water,
  With the squirrel, Adjidaumo,
  Perched and frisking on the summit.
    Full of scorn was Hiawatha
  When he saw the fish rise upward,
  Saw the pike, the Maskenozha,
  Coming nearer, nearer to him,
  And he shouted through the water,
"Esa! esa! shame upon you!
  You are but the pike, Kenozha,
  You are not the fish I wanted,
  You are not the King of Fishes!"
    Reeling downward to the bottom
  Sank the pike in great confusion,

And the mighty sturgeon, Nahma,
Said to Ugudwash, the sun-fish,
To the bream, with scales of crimson,
"Take the bait of this great boaster,
Break the line of Hiawatha!"

Slowly upward, wavering, gleaming,
Rose the Ugudwash, the sun-fish,
Seized the line of Hiawatha,
Swung with all his weight upon it,
Made a whirlpool in the water,
Whirled the birch canoe in circles,
Round and round in gurgling eddies,
Till the circles in the water
Reached the far-off sandy beaches
Till the water-flags and rushes
Nodded on the distant margins.

But when Hiawatha saw him
Slowly rising through the water,
Lifting up his disk refulgent,
Loud he shouted in derision,
"Esa! esa! shame upon you!
You are Ugudwash, the sun-fish,
You are not the fish I wanted,
You are not the King of Fishes!"

Slowly downward, wavering, gleaming,
Sank the Ugudwash, the sun-fish,
And again the sturgeon, Nahma,
Heard the shout of Hiawatha,
Heard his challenge of defiance,

The unnecessary tumult,
Ringing far across the water.

From the white sand of the bottom
Up he rose with angry gesture,
Quivering in each nerve and fibre,
Clashing all his plates of armor,
Gleaming bright with all his war-paint;
In his wrath he darted upward,
Flashing leaped into the sunshine,
Opened his great jaws, and swallowed
Both canoe and Hiawatha.

Down into that darksome cavern
Plunged the headlong Hiawatha
As a log on some black river
Shoots and plunges down the rapids,
Found himself in utter darkness,
Groped about in helpless wonder,
Till he felt a great heart beating,
Throbbing in that utter darkness.

And he smote it in his anger,
With his fist, the heart of Nahma.
Felt the mighty King of Fishes
Shudder through each nerve and fibre,
Heard the water gurgle round him
As he leaped and staggered through it,
Sick at heart, and faint and weary.

Crosswise then did Hiawatha
Drag his birch-canoe for safety,
Lest from out the jaws of Nahma,

In the turmoil and confusion,
Forth he might be hurled and perish.
And the squirrel, Adjidaumo,
Frisked and chattered very gayly,
Toiled and tugged with Hiawatha
Till the labor was completed.
Then said Hiawatha to him,
"O my little friend, the squirrel,
Bravely have you toiled to help me;
Take the thanks of Hiawatha,
And the name which now he gives you;
For hereafter and forever
Boys shall call you Adjidaumo,
Tail-in-air the boys shall call you!"
And again the sturgeon, Nahma,
Gasped and quivered in the water,
Then was still, and drifted landward
Till he grated on the pebbles,
Till the listening Hiawatha
Heard him grate upon the margin,
Felt him strand upon the pebbles,
Knew that Nahma, King of Fishes,
Lay there dead upon the margin.
Then he heard a clang and flapping,
As of many wings assembling,
Heard a screaming and confusion,
As of birds of prey contending,
Saw a gleam of light above him,
Shining through the ribs of Nahma.

Saw the glittering eyes of sea-gulls,
Of Kayoshk, the sea-gulls, peering,
Gazing at him through the opening,
Heard them saying to each other,
" ' T is our brother, Hiawatha ! "
    And he shouted from below them,
Cried exulting from the caverns :
"O ye sea-gulls ! O my brothers !
I have slain the sturgeon, Nahma ;
Make the rifts a little larger,
With your claws the openings widen,
Set me free from this dark prison,
And henceforward and forever
Men shall speak of your achievements,
Calling you Kayoshk, the sea-gulls,
Yes, Kayoshk, the Noble Scratchers ! "
    And the wild and clamorous sea-gulls
Toiled with beak and claws together,
Made the rifts and openings wider
In the mighty ribs of Nahma,
And from peril and from prison,
From the body of the sturgeon,
From the peril of the water,
They released my Hiawatha.
    He was standing near his wigwam,
On the margin of the water,
And he called to old Nokomis,
Called and beckoned to Nokomis,
Pointed to the sturgeon, Nahma,

141

Lying lifeless on the pebbles,
With the sea-gulls feeding on him.

"I have slain the Mishe-Nahma,
Slain the King of Fishes ! " said he ;
"Look ! the sea-gulls feed upon him,
Yes, my friends Kayoshk, the sea-gulls ;
Drive them not away, Nokomis,
They have saved me from great peril
In the body of the sturgeon,
Wait until their meal is ended,
Till their craws are full with feasting,
Till they homeward fly, at sunset,
To their nests among the marshes ;
Then bring all your pots and kettles,
And make oil for us in Winter."

And she waited till the sun set,
Till the pallid moon, the Night-sun.
Rose above the tranquil water,
Till Kayoshk, the sated sea-gulls,
From their banquet rose with clamor,
And across the fiery sunset
Winged their way to far-off islands,
To their nests among the rushes.

To his sleep went Hiawatha,
And Nokomis to her labor,
Toiling patient in the moonlight,
Till the sun and moon changed places,
Till the sky was red with sunrise,
And Kayoshk, the hungry sea-gulls,

Came back from the reedy islands,
Clamorous for their morning banquet.
   Three whole days and nights alternate
Old Nokomis and the sea-gulls
Stripped the oily flesh of Nahma,
Till the waves washed through the rib-bones,
Till the sea-gulls came no longer,
And upon the sands lay nothing
But the skeleton of Nahma.

THE COURTSHIP OF MILES STANDISH

THE SAILING OF THE MAYFLOWER

Just in the gray of the dawn, as the mists uprose from
    the meadows,
There was a stir and a sound in the slumbering village
    of Plymouth ;
Clanging and clicking of arms, and the order impera-
    tive, "Forward!"
Given in tone suppressed, a tramp of feet, and then
    silence.
Figures ten, in the mist, marched slowly out of the vil-
    lage.
Standish the stalwart it was, with eight of his valorous
    army,
Led by their Indian guide, by Hobomok, friend of the
    white men,
Northward marching to quell the sudden revolt of the
    savage.
Giants they seemed in the mist, or the mighty men of
    King David ;
Giants in heart they were, who believed in God and the
    Bible, —
Ay, who believed in the smiting of Midianites and Phi-
    listines.

Over them gleamed far off the crimson banners of morn-
ing;
Under them loud on the sands, the serried billows,
advancing,
Fired along the line, and in regular order retreated.

Many a mile had they marched, when at length the
village of Plymouth
Woke from its sleep, and arose, intent on its manifold
labors.
Sweet was the air and soft; and slowly the smoke from
the chimneys
Rose over roofs of thatch, and pointed steadily east-
ward;
Men came forth from the doors, and paused and talked
of the weather,
Said that the wind had changed, and was blowing fair
for the Mayflower;
Talked of their Captain's departure, and all the dangers
that menaced,
He being gone, the town, and what should be done in
his absence.
Merrily sang the birds, and the tender voices of women
Consecrated with hymns the common cares of the
household.
Out of the sea rose the sun, and the billows rejoiced at
his coming;
Beautiful were his feet on the purple tops of the moun-
tains;

Beautiful on the sails of the Mayflower riding at
    anchor,
Battered and blackened and worn by all the storms of
    the winter.
Loosely against her masts was hanging and flapping
    her canvas,
Rent by so many gales, and patched by the hands of the
    sailors.
Suddenly from her side, as the sun rose over the ocean,
Darted a puff of smoke, and floated seaward; anon
    rang
Loud over field and forest the cannon's roar, and the
    echoes
Heard and repeated the sound, the signal-gun of depar-
    ture!
Ah! but with louder echoes replied the hearts of the
    people!
Meekly, in voices subdued, the chapter was read from
    the Bible,
Meekly the prayer was begun, but ended in fervent
    entreaty!
Then from their houses in haste came forth the Pil-
    grims of Plymouth,
Men and women and children, all hurrying down to the
    sea-shore,
Eager, with tearful eyes, to say farewell to the May-
    flower,
Homeward bound o'er the sea, and leaving them here
    in the desert.

Foremost among them was Alden. All night he had
lain without slumber,
Turning and tossing about in the heat and unrest of his
fever.
He had beheld Miles Standish, who came back late from
the council,
Stalking into the room, and heard him mutter and
murmur ;
Sometimes it seemed a prayer, and sometimes it sounded
like swearing.
Once he had come to the bed, and stood there a moment
in silence ;
Then he had turned away, and said : "I will not awake
him ;
Let him sleep on, it is best ; for what is the use of more
talking ! "
Then he extinguished the light, and threw himself down
on his pallet,
Dressed as he was, and ready to start at the break of the
morning, —
Covered himself with the cloak he had worn in his cam-
paigns in Flanders, —
Slept as a soldier sleeps in his bivouac, ready for action.
But with the dawn he arose ; in the twilight Alden
beheld him
Put on his corselet of steel, and all the rest of his armor,
Buckle about his waist his trusty blade of Damascus,
Take from the corner his musket, and so stride out of
the chamber.

Often the heart of the youth had burned and yearned
    to embrace him,
Often his lips had essayed to speak, imploring for par-
    don ;
All the old friendship came back, with its tender and
    grateful emotions;
But his pride overmastered the nobler nature within
    him, —
Pride, and the sense of his wrong, and the burning fire
    of the insult.
So he beheld his friend departing in anger, but spake not,
Saw him go forth to danger, perhaps to death, and he
    spake not !
Then he arose from his bed, and heard what the people
    were saying,
Joined in the talk at the door, with Stephen and Richard
    and Gilbert,
Joined in the morning prayer, and in the reading of
    Scripture,
And, with the others, in haste went hurrying down to
    the sea-shore,
Down to the Plymouth Rock, that had been to their feet
    as a doorstep
Into a world unknown, — the corner-stone of a nation !

There with his boat was the Master, already a little
    impatient
Lest he should lose the tide, or the wind might shift to
    the eastward,

Square-built, hearty, and strong, with an odor of ocean
about him,
Speaking with this one and that, and cramming letters
and parcels
Into his pockets capacious, and messages mingled to-
gether
Into his narrow brain, till at last he was wholly bewil-
dered.
Nearer the boat stood Alden, with one foot placed on
the gunwale,
One still firm on the rock, and talking at times with the
sailors,
Seated erect on the thwarts, all ready and eager for
starting.
He too was eager to go, and thus put an end to his
anguish,
Thinking to fly from despair, that swifter than keel is
or canvas,
Thinking to drown in the sea the ghost that would rise
and pursue him.
But as he gazed on the crowd, he beheld the form of
Priscilla
Standing dejected among them, unconscious of all that
was passing.
Fixed were her eyes upon his, as if she divined his in-
tention,
Fixed with a look so sad, so reproachful, imploring, and
patient,

That with a sudden revulsion his heart recoiled from its
purpose,

As from the verge of a crag, where one step more is de-
struction.

Strange is the heart of man, with its quick, mysterious
instincts!

Strange is the life of man, and fatal or fated are mo-
ments,

Whereupon turn, as on hinges, the gates of the wall
adamantine!

"Here I remain!" he exclaimed, as he looked at the
heavens above him,

Thanking the Lord whose breath had scattered the mist
and the madness,

Wherein, blind and lost, to death he was staggering
headlong.

"Yonder snow-white cloud, that floats in the ether
above me,

Seems like a hand that is pointing and beckoning over
the ocean.

There is another hand, that is not so spectral and ghost-
like,

Holding me, drawing me back, and clasping mine for
protection.

Float, O hand of cloud, and vanish away in the
ether!

Roll thyself up like a fist, to threaten and daunt me; I
heed not

Either your warning or menace, or any omen of evil!

There is no land so sacred, no air so pure and so whole-
    some,
As is the air she breathes, and the soil that is pressed by
    her footsteps.
Here for her sake will I stay, and like an invisible pre-
    sence
Hover around her forever, protecting, supporting her
    weakness ;
Yes ! as my foot was the first that stepped on this rock
    at the landing,
So, with the blessing of God, shall it be the last at the
    leaving ! ''

Meanwhile the Master alert, but with dignified air
    and important,
Scanning with watchful eye the tide and the wind and
    the weather,
Walked about on the sands, and the people crowded
    around him
Saying a few last words, and enforcing his careful re-
    membrance.
Then, taking each by the hand, as if he were grasping
    a tiller,
Into the boat he sprang, and in haste shoved off to his
    vessel,
Glad in his heart to get rid of all this worry and
    flurry,
Glad to be gone from a land of sand and sickness and
    sorrow,

Short allowance of victual, and plenty of nothing but
    Gospel!
Lost in the sound of the oars was the last farewell of
    the Pilgrims.
O strong hearts and true! not one went back in the
    Mayflower!
No, not one looked back, who had set his hand to this
    ploughing!

Soon were heard on board the shouts and songs of
    the sailors
Heaving the windlass round, and hoisting the ponder-
    ous anchor.
Then the yards were braced, and all sails set to the
    west-wind,
Blowing steady and strong ; and the Mayflower sailed
    from the harbor,
Rounded the point of the Gurnet, and leaving far to the
    southward
Island and cape of sand, and the Field of the First
    Encounter,
Took the wind on her quarter, and stood for the open
    Atlantic,
Borne on the send of the sea, and the swelling hearts
    of the Pilgrims.

Long in silence they watched the receding sail of the
    vessel,
Much endeared to them all, as something living and
    human ;

Then, as if filled with the spirit, and wrapt in a vision
    prophetic,
Baring his hoary head, the excellent Elder of Plymouth
Said, "Let us pray!" and they prayed, and thanked
    the Lord and took courage.
Mournfully sobbed the waves at the base of the rock,
    and above them
Bowed and whispered the wheat on the hill of death,
    and their kindred
Seemed to awake in their graves, and to join in the
    prayer that they uttered.
Sun-illumined and white, on the eastern verge of the
    ocean
Gleamed the departing sail, like a marble slab in a
    graveyard;
Buried beneath it lay forever all hope of escaping.
Lo! as they turned to depart, they saw the form of an
    Indian,
Watching them from the hill; but while they spake
    with each other,
Pointing with outstretched hands, and saying, "Look!"
    he had vanished.
So they returned to their homes; but Alden lingered a
    little,
Musing alone on the shore, and watching the wash of
    the billows
Round the base of the rock, and the sparkle and flash
    of the sunshine,
Like the spirit of God, moving visibly over the waters.

THE SEASIDE AND THE FIRESIDE

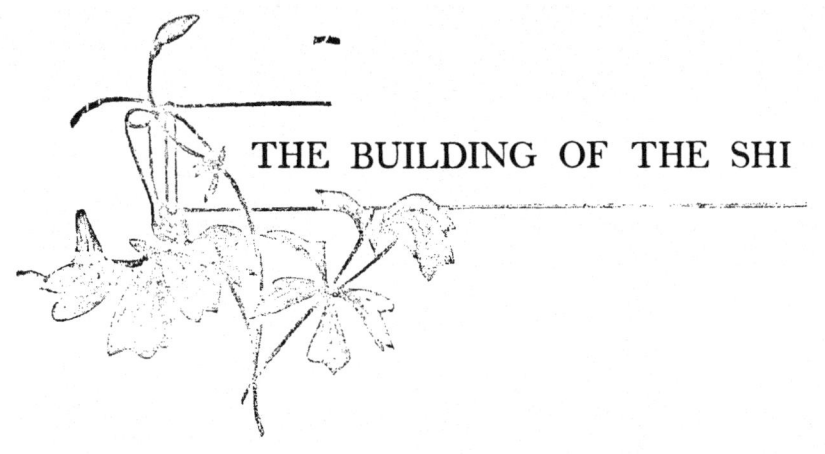

" BUILD me straight, O worthy Master !
　　Stanch and strong, a goodly vessel,
　That shall laugh at all disaster,
　　And with wave and whirlwind wrestle ! "

　The merchant's word
　Delighted the Master heard ;
　For his heart was in his work, and the heart
　Giveth grace unto every Art.
　A quiet smile played round his lips,
　As the eddies and dimples of the tide
　Play round the bows of ships,
　That steadily at anchor ride.
　And with a voice that was full of glee,
　He answered, " Erelong we will launch
　A vessel as goodly, and strong, and stanch,
　As ever weathered a wintry sea ! "
　And first with nicest skill and art,
　Perfect and finished in every part,

A little model the Master wrought,
Which should be to the larger plan
What the child is to the man,
Its counterpart in miniature ;
That with a hand more swift and sure
The greater labor might be brought
To answer to his inward thought.
And as he labored, his mind ran o'er
The various ships that were built of yore,
And above them all, and strangest of all
Towered the Great Harry, crank and tall,
Whose picture was hanging on the wall,
With bows and stern raised high in air,
And balconies hanging here and there,
And signal lanterns and flags afloat,
And eight round towers, like those that frown
From some old castle, looking down
Upon the drawbridge and the moat.
And he said with a smile, "Our ship, I wis,
Shall be of another form than this ! "
It was of another form, indeed ;
Built for freight, and yet for speed,
A beautiful and gallant craft ;
Broad in the beam, that the stress of the blast,
Pressing down upon sail and mast,
Might not the sharp bows overwhelm ;
Broad in the beam, but sloping aft
With graceful curve and slow degrees,
That she might be docile to the helm,

And that the currents of parted seas,
Closing behind, with mighty force,
Might aid and not impede her course.

In the ship-yard stood the Master,
With the model of the vessel,
That should laugh at all disaster,
And with wave and whirlwind wrestle !

Covering many a rood of ground,
Lay the timber piled around ;
Timber of chestnut, and elm, and oak,
And scattered here and there, with these,
The knarred and crooked cedar knees ;
Brought from regions far away,
From Pascagoula's sunny bay,
And the banks of the roaring Roanoke !
Ah ! what a wondrous thing it is
To note how many wheels of toil
One thought, one word, can set in motion !
There 's not a ship that sails the ocean,
But every climate, every soil,
Must bring its tribute, great or small
And help to build the wooden wall !

The sun was rising o'er the sea,
And long the level shadows lay,
As if they, too, the beams would be
Of some great, airy argosy,

Framed and launched in a single day.
That silent architect, the sun,
Had hewn and laid them every one,
Ere the work of man was yet begun.
Beside the Master, when he spoke,
A youth, against an anchor leaning,
Listened, to catch his slightest meaning.
Only the long waves, as they broke
In ripples on the pebbly beach,
Interrupted the old man's speech.

Beautiful they were, in sooth,
The old man and the fiery youth !
The old man, in whose busy brain
Many a ship that sailed the main
Was modelled o'er and o'er again ; —
The fiery youth, who was to be
The heir of his dexterity,
The heir of his house, and his daughter's hand,
When he had built and launched from land
What the elder head had planned.

" Thus," said he, " will we build this ship !
Lay square the blocks upon the slip,
And follow well this plan of mine.
Choose the timbers with greatest care ;
Of all that is unsound beware ;
For only what is sound and strong
To this vessel shall belong.

The sun shone on her golden hair,
And her cheek was glowing fresh and fair

Cedar of Maine and Georgia pine
Here together shall combine.
A goodly frame, and a goodly fame,
And the Union be her name !
For the day that gives her to the sea
Shall give my daughter unto thee ! "

The Master's word
Enraptured the young man heard ;
And as he turned his face aside,
With a look of joy and a thrill of pride,
Standing before
Her father's door,
He saw the form of his promised bride.
The sun shone on her golden hair,
And her cheek was glowing fresh and fair,
With the breath of morn and the soft sea air.
Like a beauteous barge was she,
Still at rest on the sandy beach,
Just beyond the billow's reach ;
But he
Was the restless, seething, stormy sea !

Ah, how skilful grows the hand
That obeyeth Love's command !
It is the heart, and not the brain,
That to the highest doth attain,
And he who followeth Love's behest
Far excelleth all the rest !

Thus with the rising of the sun
Was the noble task begun,
And soon throughout the ship-yard's bounds
Were heard the intermingled sounds
Of axes and of mallets, plied
With vigorous arms on every side;
Plied so deftly and so well,
That, ere the shadows of evening fell,
The keel of oak for a noble ship,
Scarfed and bolted, straight and strong,
Was lying ready, and stretched along
The blocks, well placed upon the slip.
Happy, thrice happy, every one
Who sees his labor well begun,
And not perplexed and multiplied,
By idly waiting for time and tide !

And when the hot, long day was o'er,
The young man at the Master's door
Sat with the maiden calm and still,
And within the porch, a little more
Removed beyond the evening chill,
The father sat, and told them tales
Of wrecks in the great September gales,
Of pirates coasting the Spanish Main,
And ships that never came back again,
The chance and change of a sailor's life,
Want and plenty, rest and strife,
His roving fancy, like the wind,

That nothing can stay and nothing can bind,
And the magic charm of foreign lands,
With shadows of palms, and shining sands,
Where the tumbling surf,
O'er the coral reefs of Madagascar,
Washes the feet of the swarthy Lascar,
As he lies alone and asleep on the turf.
And the trembling maiden held her breath
At the tales of that awful, pitiless sea,
With all its terror and mystery,
The dim, dark sea, so like unto Death,
That divides and yet unites mankind !
And whenever the old man paused, a gleam
From the bowl of his pipe would awhile illume
The silent group in the twilight gloom,
And thoughtful faces, as in a dream ;
And for a moment one might mark
What had been hidden by the dark,
That the head of the maiden lay at rest,
Tenderly, on the young man's breast !

Day by day the vessel grew,
With timbers fashioned strong and true,
Stemson and keelson and sternson-knee,
Till, framed with perfect symmetry,
A skeleton ship rose up to view !
And around the bows and along the side
The heavy hammers and mallets plied,
Till after many a week, at length,

Wonderful for form and strength,
Sublime in its enormous bulk,
Loomed aloft the shadowy hulk !
And around it columns of smoke, upwreathing,
Rose from the boiling, bubbling, seething
Caldron, that glowed,
And overflowed
With the black tar, heated for the sheathing.
And amid the clamors
Of clattering hammers,
He who listened heard now and then
The song of the Master and his men : —

"Build me straight, O worthy Master,
   Stanch and strong, a goodly vessel,
That shall laugh at all disaster,
   And with wave and whirlwind wrestle !"

With oaken brace and copper band,
Lay the rudder on the sand,
That, like a thought, should have control
Over the movement of the whole ;
And near it the anchor, whose giant hand
Would reach down and grapple with the land,
And immovable and fast
Hold the great ship against the bellowing blast !
And at the bows an image stood,
By a cunning artist carved in wood,
With robes of white, that far behind

Seemed to be fluttering in the wind.
It was not shaped in a classic mould,
Not like a Nymph or Goddess of old,
Or Naiad rising from the water,
But modelled from the Master's daughter !
On many a dreary and misty night,
'T will be seen by the rays of the signal light,
Speeding along through the rain and the dark,
Like a ghost in its snow-white sark,
The pilot of some phantom bark,
Guiding the vessel, in its flight,
By a path none other knows aright !

Behold, at last,
Each tall and tapering mast
Is swung into its place ;
Shrouds and stays
Holding it firm and fast !

Long ago,
In the deer-haunted forests of Maine,
When upon mountain and plain
Lay the snow,
They fell, — those lordly pines !
Those grand, majestic pines !
'Mid shouts and cheers
The jaded steers,
Panting beneath the goad,
Dragged down the weary, winding road

Those captive kings so straight and tall,
To be shorn of their streaming hair,
And naked and bare,
To feel the stress and the strain
Of the wind and the reeling main,
Whose roar
Would remind them forevermore
Of their native forests they should not see again.

And everywhere
The slender, graceful spars
Poise aloft in the air,
And at the mast-head,
White, blue, and red,
A flag unrolls the stripes and stars.
Ah ! when the wanderer, lonely, friendless,
In foreign harbors shall behold
That flag unrolled,
'T will be as a friendly hand
Stretched out from his native land,
Filling his heart with memories sweet and endless !

All is finished ! and at length
Has come the bridal day
Of beauty and of strength.
To-day the vessel shall be launched !
With fleecy clouds the sky is blanched,
And o'er the bay,

Slowly, in all its splendors dight,
The great sun rises to behold the sight.

The ocean old,
Centuries old,
Strong as youth, and as uncontrolled,
Paces restless to and fro,
Up and down the sands of gold.
His beating heart is not at rest ;
And far and wide,
With ceaseless flow,
His beard of snow
Heaves with the heaving of his breast.
He waits impatient for his bride.
There she stands,
With her foot upon the sands,
Decked with flags and streamers gay,
In honor of her marriage day,
Her snow-white signals fluttering, blending,
Round her like a veil descending
Ready to be
The bride of the gray old sea.

On the deck another bride
Is standing by her lover's side.
Shadows from the flags and shrouds,
Like the shadows cast by clouds,
Broken by many a sudden fleck,
Fall around them on the deck.

The prayer is said,
The service read,
The joyous bridegroom bows his head ;
And in tears the good old Master
Shakes the brown hand of his son
Kisses his daughter's glowing cheek
In silence, for he cannot speak,
And ever faster
Down his own the tears begin to run.
The worthy pastor —
The shepherd of that wandering flock,
That has the ocean for its wold,
That has the vessel for its fold,
Leaping ever from rock to rock —
Spake, with accents mild and clear,
Words of warning, words of cheer,
But tedious to the bridegroom's ear.
He knew the chart
Of the sailor's heart,
All its pleasures and its griefs,
All its shallows and rocky reefs,
All those secret currents, that flow
With such resistless undertow,
And lift and drift, with terrible force,
The will from its moorings and its course.
Therefore he spake, and thus said he : —
" Like unto ships far off at sea,
Outward or homeward bound, are we.
Before, behind, and all around,

Floats and swings the horizon's bound,
Seems at its distant rim to rise
And climb the crystal wall of the skies,
And then again to turn and sink,
As if we could slide from its outer brink.
Ah ! it is not the sea,
It is not the sea that sinks and shelves,
But ourselves
That rock and rise
With endless and uneasy motion,
Now touching the very skies,
Now sinking into the depths of ocean.
Ah ! if our souls but poise and swing
Like the compass in its brazen ring,
Ever level and ever true
To the toil and the task we have to do,
We shall sail securely, and safely reach
The Fortunate Isles, on whose shining beach
The sights we see, and the sounds we hear,
Will be those of joy and not of fear ! "

Then the Master,
With a gesture of command,
Waved his hand ;
And at the word,
Loud and sudden there was heard,
All around them and below,
The sound of hammers, blow on blow,
Knocking away the shores and spurs.

And see ! she stirs !
She starts, — she moves, — she seems to feel
The thrill of life along her keel,
And, spurning with her foot the ground,
With one exulting, joyous bound,
She leaps into the ocean's arms !

And lo ! from the assembled crowd
There rose a shout, prolonged and loud,
That to the ocean seemed to say,
"Take her, O bridegroom, old and gray,
Take her to thy protecting arms,
With all her youth and all her charms !"

How beautiful she is ! How fair
She lies within those arms, that press
Her form with many a soft caress
Of tenderness and watchful care !
Sail forth into the sea, O ship !
Through wind and wave, right onward steer !
The moistened eye, the trembling lip,
Are not the signs of doubt or fear.

Sail forth into the sea of life,
O gentle, loving, trusting wife,
And safe from all adversity
Upon the bosom of that sea
Thy comings and thy goings be !
For gentleness and love and trust

Prevail o'er angry wave and gust ;
And in the wreck of noble lives
Something immortal still survives !

Thou, too, sail on, O Ship of State !
Sail on, O UNION, strong and great !
Humanity with all its fears,
With all the hopes of future years,
Is hanging breathless on thy fate !
We know what Master laid thy keel,
What Workmen wrought thy ribs of steel,
Who made each mast, and sail, and rope,
What anvils rang, what hammers beat,
In what a forge and what a heat
Were shaped the anchors of thy hope !
Fear not each sudden sound and shock,
'T is of the wave and not the rock ;
'T is but the flapping of the sail,
And not a rent made by the gale !
In spite of rock and tempest's roar,
In spite of false lights on the shore,
Sail on, nor fear to breast the sea !
Our hearts, our hopes, are all with thee,
Our hearts, our hopes, our prayers, our tears,
Our faith triumphant o'er our fears,
Are all with thee, — are all with thee !

THE SECRET OF THE SEA

Ah ! what pleasant visions haunt me
  As I gaze upon the sea !
All the old romantic legends,
  All my dreams, come back to me.

Sails of silk and ropes of sandal,
  Such as gleam in ancient lore ;
And the singing of the sailors,
  And the answer from the shore !

Most of all, the Spanish ballad
  Haunts me oft, and tarries long,
Of the noble Count Arnaldos
  And the sailor's mystic song.

Like the long waves on a sea-beach,
  Where the sand as silver shines,
With a soft, monotonous cadence,
  Flow its unrhymed lyric lines ; —

Telling how the Count Arnaldos,
  With his hawk upon his hand,
Saw a fair and stately galley,
  Steering onward to the land ; —

How he heard the ancient helmsman
    Chant a song so wild and clear,
That the sailing sea-bird slowly
    Poised upon the mast to hear,

Till his soul was full of longing,
    And he cried, with impulse strong, —
" Helmsman ! for the love of heaven,
    Teach me, too, that wondrous song ! "

" Wouldst thou," — so the helmsman answered,
    " Learn the secret of the sea ?
Only those who brave its dangers
    Comprehend its mystery ! "

In each sail that skims the horizon,
    In each landward-blowing breeze,
I behold that stately galley,
    Hear those mournful melodies ;

Till my soul is full of longing
    For the secret of the sea,
And the heart of the great ocean
    Sends a thrilling pulse through me.

TWILIGHT

THE twilight is sad and cloudy,
　　The wind blows wild and free,
And like the wings of sea-birds
　　Flash the white caps of the sea.

But in the fisherman's cottage
　　There shines a ruddier light,
And a little face at the window
　　Peers out into the night.

Close, close it is pressed to the window,
　　As if those childish eyes
Were looking into the darkness
　　To see some form arise.

And a woman's waving shadow
　　Is passing to and fro,
Now rising to the ceiling,
　　Now bowing and bending low.

What tale do the roaring ocean,
　　And the night-wind, bleak and wild,
As they beat at the crazy casement,
　　Tell to that little child?

And why do the roaring ocean,
   And the night-wind, wild and bleak,
As they beat at the heart of the mother
   Drive the color from her cheek ?

SIR HUMPHREY GILBERT

Southward with fleet of ice
  Sailed the corsair Death;
Wild and fast blew the blast,
  And the east-wind was his breath.

His lordly ships of ice
  Glisten in the sun;
On each side, like pennons wide
  Flashing crystal streamlets run.

His sails of white sea-mist
  Dripped with silver rain;
But where he passed there were cast
  Leaden shadows o'er the main.

Eastward from Campobello
  Sir Humphrey Gilbert sailed;
Three days or more seaward he bore,
  Then, alas! the land-wind failed.

Alas! the land-wind failed,
  And ice-cold grew the night;
And nevermore, on sea or shore,
  Should Sir Humphrey see the light.

He sat upon the deck,
  The Book was in his hand;
"Do not fear! Heaven is as near,"
  He said, "by water as by land!"

In the first watch of the night,
  Without a signal's sound,
Out of the sea, mysteriously,
  The fleet of Death rose all around.

The moon and the evening star
  Were hanging in the shrouds;
Every mast, as it passed,
  Seemed to rake the passing clouds.

They grappled with their prize,
  At midnight black and cold!
As of a rock was the shock;
  Heavily the ground-swell rolled.

Southward through day and dark,
  They drift in close embrace,
With mist and rain, o'er the open main;
  Yet there seems no change of place.

Southward, forever southward,
  They drift through dark and day;
And like a dream, in the Gulf-Stream
  Sinking, vanish all away.

THE LIGHTHOUSE

The rocky ledge runs far into the sea,
  And on its outer point, some miles away,
The Lighthouse lifts its massive masonry,
  A pillar of fire by night, of cloud by day.

Even at this distance I can see the tides,
  Upheaving, break unheard along its base,
A speechless wrath, that rises and subsides
  In the white lip and tremor of the face.

And as the evening darkens, lo ! how bright,
  Through the deep purple of the twilight air,
Beams forth the sudden radiance of its light
  With strange, unearthly splendor in the glare !

Not one alone ; from each projecting cape
  And perilous reef along the ocean's verge,
Starts into life a dim, gigantic shape,
  Holding its lantern o'er the restless surge.

Like the great giant Christopher it stands
  Upon the brink of the tempestuous wave
Wading far out among the rocks and sands,
  The night-o'ertaken mariner to save.

THE LIGHTHOUSE

And the great ships sail outward and return,
  Bending and bowing o'er the billowy swells
And ever joyful, as they see it burn,
  They wave their silent welcomes and farewells.

They come forth from the darkness, and their sails
  Gleam for a moment only in the blaze,
And eager faces, as the light unveils,
  Gaze at the tower, and vanish while they gaze.

The mariner remembers when a child,
  On his first voyage, he saw it fade and sink ;
And when, returning from adventures wild,
  He saw it rise again o'er ocean's brink.

Steadfast, serene, immovable, the same
  Year after year, through all the silent night
Burns on forevermore that quenchless flame,
  Shines on that inextinguishable light !

It sees the ocean to its bosom clasp
  The rocks and sea-sand with the kiss of peace ;
It sees the wild winds lift it in their grasp,
  And hold it up, and shake it like a fleece.

The startled waves leap over it; the storm
  Smites it with all the scourges of the rain
And steadily against its solid form
  Press the great shoulders of the hurricane.

The sea-bird wheeling round it, with the din
    Of wings and winds and solitary cries,
Blinded and maddened by the light within,
    Dashes himself against the glare, and dies.

A new Prometheus, chained upon the rock,
    Still grasping in his hand the fire of Jove,
It does not hear the cry, nor heed the shock,
    But hails the mariner with words of love.

" Sail on ! " it says, "sail on, ye stately ships!
    And with your floating bridge the ocean span;
Be mine to guard this light from all eclipse,
    Be yours to bring man nearer unto man ! "

THE BUILDERS

ALL are architects of Fate,
  Working in these walls of Time ;
Some with massive deeds and great,
  Some with ornaments of rhyme.

Nothing useless is, or low ;
  Each thing in its place is best ;
And what seems but idle show
  Strengthens and supports the rest.

For the structure that we raise,
  Time is with materials filled ;
Our to-days and yesterdays
  Are the blocks with which we build.

Truly shape and fashion these ;
  Leave no yawning gaps between ;
Think not, because no man sees,
  Such things will remain unseen.

In the elder days of Art,
  Builders wrought with greatest care
Each minute and unseen part ;
  For the Gods see everywhere.

THE BUILDERS

Let us do our work as well,
　Both the unseen and the seen ;
Make the house, where Gods may dwell,
　Beautiful, entire, and clean.

Else our lives are incomplete,
　Standing in these walls of Time,
Broken stairways, where the feet
　Stumble as they seek to climb.

Build to-day, then, strong and sure,
　With a firm and ample base ;
And ascending and secure
　Shall to-morrow find its place.

Thus alone can we attain
　To those turrets, where the eye
Sees the world as one vast plain,
　And one boundless reach of sky.

GASPAR BECERRA

By his evening fire the artist
    Pondered o'er his secret shame;
Baffled, weary, and disheartened,
    Still he mused, and dreamed of fame.

'T was an image of the Virgin
    That had tasked his utmost skill;
But, alas! his fair ideal
    Vanished and escaped him still.

From a distant Eastern island
    Had the precious wood been brought;
Day and night the anxious master
    At his toil untiring wrought;

Till, discouraged and desponding,
    Sat he now in shadows deep,
And the day's humiliation
    Found oblivion in sleep.

Then a voice cried, "Rise, O master!
    From the burning brand of oak
Shape the thought that stirs within thee!"—
    And the startled artist woke, —

Woke, and from the smoking embers
    Seized and quenched the glowing wood;
And therefrom he carved an image,
    And he saw that it was good.

O thou sculptor, painter, poet!
    Take this lesson to thy heart:
That is best which lieth nearest;
    Shape from that thy work of art.

PEGASUS IN POUND

Once into a quiet village,
 Without haste and without heed
In the golden prime of morning,
 Strayed the poet's wingèd steed.

It was Autumn, and incessant
 Piped the quails from shocks and sheaves,
And, like living coals, the apples
 Burned among the withering leaves.

Loud the clamorous bell was ringing
 From its belfry gaunt and grim ;
'T was the daily call to labor,
 Not a triumph meant for him.

Not the less he saw the landscape,
 In its gleaming vapor veiled ;
Not the less he breathed the odors
 That the dying leaves exhaled.

Thus, upon the village common,
 By the school-boys he was found ;
And the wise men, in their wisdom,
 Put him straightway into pound.

185

Then the sombre village crier,
  Ringing loud his brazen bell,
Wandered down the street proclaiming
  There was an estray to sell.

And the curious country people,
  Rich and poor, and young and old,
Came in haste to see this wondrous
  Wingèd steed, with mane of gold.

Thus the day passed, and the evening
  Fell, with vapors cold and dim ;
But it brought no food nor shelter,
  Brought no straw nor stall, for him.

Patiently, and still expectant,
  Looked he through the wooden bars,
Saw the moon rise o'er the landscape,
  Saw the tranquil, patient stars ;

Till at length the bell at midnight
  Sounded from its dark abode,
And, from out a neighboring farm-yard,
  Loud the cock Alectryon crowed.

Then, with nostrils wide distended,
  Breaking from his iron chain,
And unfolding far his pinions,
  To those stars he soared again.

On the morrow, when the village
   Woke to all its toil and care,
Lo! the strange steed had departed,
   And they knew not when nor where.

But they found, upon the greensward
   Where his struggling hoofs had trod,
Pure and bright, a fountain flowing
   From the hoof-marks in the sod.

From that hour, the fount unfailing
   Gladdens the whole region round,
Strengthening all who drink its waters,
   While it soothes them with its sound.

BIRDS OF PASSAGE

THE PHANTOM SHIP

In Mather's Magnalia Christi,
    Of the old colonial time,
May be found in prose the legend
    That is here set down in rhyme.

A ship sailed from New Haven
    And the keen and frosty airs,
That filled her sails at parting,
    Were heavy with good men's prayers.

" O Lord! if it be thy pleasure " —
    Thus prayed the old divine —
" To bury our friends in the ocean,
    Take them, for they are thine ! "

But Master Lamberton muttered,
    And under his breath said he,
" This ship is so crank and walty,
    I fear our grave she will be!"

And the ships that came from England,
  When the winter months were gone,
Brought no tidings of this vessel
  Nor of Master Lamberton.

This put the people to praying
  That the Lord would let them hear
What in his greater wisdom
  He had done with friends so dear.

And at last their prayers were answered
  It was in the month of June,
An hour before the sunset
  Of a windy afternoon,

When, steadily steering landward,
  A ship was seen below,
And they knew it was Lamberton, Master,
  Who sailed so long ago.

On she came, with a cloud of canvas,
  Right against the wind that blew,
Until the eye could distinguish
  The faces of the crew.

Then fell her straining topmasts,
  Hanging tangled in the shrouds,
And her sails were loosened and lifted,
  And blown away like clouds.

And the masts, with all their rigging,
   Fell slowly, one by one,
And the hulk dilated and vanished,
   As a sea-mist in the sun !

And the people who saw this marvel
   Each said unto his friend,
That this was the mould of their vessel,
   And thus her tragic end.

And the pastor of the village
   Gave thanks to God in prayer,
That, to quiet their troubled spirits,
   He had sent this Ship of Air.

THE WARDEN OF THE CINQUE PORTS

A MIST was driving down the British Channel,
  The day was just begun
And through the window-panes, on floor and panel,
  Streamed the red autumn sun.

It glanced on flowing flag and rippling pennon,
  And the white sails of ships ;
And, from the frowning rampart, the black cannon
  Hailed it with feverish lips.

Sandwich and Romney, Hastings, Hithe, and Dover
  Were all alert that day,
To see the French war-steamers speeding over,
  When the fog cleared away.

Sullen and silent, and like couchant lions,
  Their cannon, through the night,
Holding their breath, had watched, in grim defiance,
  The sea-coast opposite.

And now they roared at drum-beat from their stations
  On every citadel ;
Each answering each, with morning salutations,
  That all was well.

And down the coast, all taking up the burden,
 Replied the distant forts,
As if to summon from his sleep the Warden
 And Lord of the Cinque Ports.

Him shall no sunshine from the fields of azure,
 No drum-beat from the wall,
No morning gun from the black fort's embrasure,
 Awaken with its call!

No more, surveying with an eye impartial
 The long line of the coast,
Shall the gaunt figure of the old Field Marshal
 Be seen upon his post!

For in the night, unseen, a single warrior,
 In sombre harness mailed,
Dreaded of man, and surnamed the Destroyer,
 The rampart wall had scaled.

He passed into the chamber of the sleeper,
 The dark and silent room,
And as he entered, darker grew, and deeper,
 The silence and the gloom.

He did not pause to parley or dissemble,
 But smote the Warden hoar;
Ah! what a blow! that made all England tremble
 And groan from shore to shore.

Meanwhile, without, the surly cannon waited,
    The sun rose bright o'erhead ;
Nothing in Nature's aspect intimated
    That a great man was dead.

THE EMPEROR'S BIRD'S-NEST

Once the Emperor Charles of Spain,
  With his swarthy, grave commanders,
I forget in what campaign,
Long besieged, in mud and rain,
  Some old frontier town of Flanders.

Up and down the dreary camp,
  In great boots of Spanish leather,
Striding with a measured tramp,
These Hidalgos, dull and damp,
  Cursed the Frenchmen, cursed the weather.

Thus as to and fro they went
  Over upland and through hollow,
Giving their impatience vent,
Perched upon the Emperor's tent,
  In her nest, they spied a swallow.

Yes, it was a swallow's nest,
  Built of clay and hair of horses
Mane, or tail, or dragoon's crest,
Found on hedge-rows east and west,
  After skirmish of the forces.

197

Then an old Hidalgo said,
 As he twirled his gray mustachio,
"Sure this swallow overhead
Thinks the Emperor's tent a shed,
 And the Emperor but a Macho!"

Hearing his imperial name
 Coupled with those words of malice,
Half in anger, half in shame,
Forth the great campaigner came
 Slowly from his canvas palace.

"Let no hand the bird molest,"
 Said he solemnly, "nor hurt her!"
Adding then, by way of jest,
"Golondrina is my guest,
 'T is the wife of some deserter!"

Swift as bowstring speeds a shaft,
 Through the camp was spread the rumor,
And the soldiers, as they quaffed
Flemish beer at dinner, laughed
 At the Emperor's pleasant humor.

So unharmed and unafraid
 Sat the swallow still and brooded,
Till the constant cannonade
Through the walls a breach had made,
 And the siege was thus concluded.

Then the army, elsewhere bent,
  Struck its tents as if disbanding,
Only not the Emperor's tent,
For he ordered, ere he went,
  Very curtly, " Leave it standing ! "

So it stood there all alone,
  Loosely flapping, torn and tattered,
Till the brood was fledged and flown,
Singing o'er those walls of stone
  Which the cannon-shot had shattered.

VICTOR GALBRAITH

Under the walls of Monterey
At daybreak the bugles began to play,
  Victor Galbraith !
In the mist of the morning damp and gray,
These were the words they seemed to say ·
  "Come forth to thy death,
  Victor Galbraith !"

Forth he came, with a martial tread ;
Firm was his step, erect his head ;
  Victor Galbraith,
He who so well the bugle played,
Could not mistake the words it said ·
  " Come forth to thy death,
  Victor Galbraith ! "

He looked at the earth, he looked at the sky,
He looked at the files of musketry,
  Victor Galbraith !
And he said, with a steady voice and eye,
"Take good aim ; I am ready to die !"
  Thus challenges death
  Victor Galbraith.

Twelve fiery tongues flashed straight and red,
Six leaden balls on their errand sped ;
  Victor Galbraith

Falls to the ground, but he is not dead :
His name was not stamped on those balls of lead,
   And they only scath
    Victor Galbraith.

Three balls are in his breast and brain,
But he rises out of the dust again,
    Victor Galbraith !
The water he drinks has a bloody stain ;
" Oh kill me, and put me out of my pain ! "
   In his agony prayeth
    Victor Galbraith.

Forth dart once more those tongues of flame,
And the bugler has died a death of shame,
    Victor Galbraith !
His soul has gone back to whence it came,
And no one answers to the name,
   When the Sergeant saith,
    " Victor Galbraith ! "

Under the walls of Monterey
By night a bugle is heard to play,
    Victor Galbraith !
Through the mist of the valley damp and gray
The sentinels hear the sound and say,
   " That is the wraith
    Of Victor Galbraith ! "

MY LOST YOUTH

OFTEN I think of the beautiful town
　　That is seated by the sea ;
Often in thought go up and down
The pleasant streets of that dear old town,
　　And my youth comes back to me.
　　　　And a verse of a Lapland song
　　　　Is haunting my memory still :
　　　　" A boy's will is the wind's will,
And the thoughts of youth are long, long thoughts."

I can see the shadowy lines of its trees,
　　And catch, in sudden gleams,
The sheen of the far-surrounding seas,
And islands that were the Hesperides
　　Of all my boyish dreams.
　　　　And the burden of that old song,
　　　　It murmurs and whispers still:
　　　　" A boy's will is the wind's will,
And the thoughts of youth are long, long thoughts."

I remember the black wharves and the slips,
　　And the sea-tides tossing free ;
And Spanish sailors with bearded lips,
And the beauty and mystery of the ships,
　　And the magic of the sea.

And the voice of that wayward song
Is singing and saying still:
"A boy's will is the wind's will,
And the thoughts of youth are long, long thoughts."

I remember the bulwarks by the shore,
  And the fort upon the hill;
The sunrise gun, with its hollow roar,
The drum-beat repeated o'er and o'er,
  And the bugle wild and shrill.
    And the music of that old song
    Throbs in my memory still:
    "A boy's will is the wind's will,
And the thoughts of youth are long, long thoughts."

I remember the sea-fight far away,
  How it thundered o'er the tide!
And the dead captains, as they lay
In their graves, o'erlooking the tranquil bay
  Where they in battle died.
    And the sound of that mournful song
    Goes through me with a thrill:
    "A boy's will is the wind's will,
And the thoughts of youth are long, long thoughts.

I can see the breezy dome of groves,
  The shadows of Deering's Woods;
And the friendships old and the early loves
Come back with a Sabbath sound, as of doves
  In quiet neighborhoods.

And the verse of that sweet old song,
  It flutters and murmurs still ·
"A boy's will is the wind's will,
And the thoughts of youth are long, long thoughts."

I remember the gleams and glooms that dart
  Across the school-boy's brain ;
The song and the silence in the heart,
That in part are prophecies, and in part
  Are longings wild and vain.
    And the voice of that fitful song
    Sings on, and is never still:
    "A boy's will is the wind's will,
And the thoughts of youth are long, long thoughts."

There are things of which I may not speak ;
  There are dreams that cannot die ;
There are thoughts that make the strong heart weak,
And bring a pallor into the cheek,
  And a mist before the eye.
    And the words of that fatal song
    Come over me like a chill :
    "A boy's will is the wind's will,
And the thoughts of youth are long, long thoughts."

Strange to me now are the forms I meet
  When I visit the dear old town ;
But the native air is pure and sweet,
And the trees that o'ershadow each well-known street,

As they balance up and down,
Are singing the beautiful song,
Are sighing and whispering still :
" A boy's will is the wind's will,
And the thoughts of youth are long, long thoughts."

And Deering's Woods are fresh and fair,
And with joy that is almost pain
My heart goes back to wander there,
And among the dreams of the days that were,
I find my lost youth again.
And the strange and beautiful song,
The groves are repeating it still ·
" A boy's will is the wind's will,
And the thoughts of youth are long, long thoughts."

THE ROPEWALK

In that building, long and low,
With its windows all a-row,
   Like the port-holes of a hulk,
Human spiders spin and spin,
Backward down their threads so thin
   Dropping, each a hempen bulk.

At the end, an open door ;
Squares of sunshine on the floor
   Light the long and dusky lane ;
And the whirring of a wheel,
Dull and drowsy, makes me feel
   All its spokes are in my brain.

As the spinners to the end
Downward go and reascend,
   Gleam the long threads in the sun ;
While within this brain of mine
Cobwebs brighter and more fine
   By the busy wheel are spun.

Two fair maidens in a swing,
Like white doves upon the wing
   First before my vision pass ;

Laughing, as their gentle hands
Closely clasp the twisted strands,
   At their shadow on the grass.

Then a booth of mountebanks,
With its smell of tan and planks,
   And a girl poised high in air
On a cord, in spangled dress,
With a faded loveliness,
   And a weary look of care.

Then a homestead among farms,
And a woman with bare arms
   Drawing water from a well ;
As the bucket mounts apace,
With it mounts her own fair face,
   As at some magician's spell.

Then an old man in a tower,
Ringing loud the noontide hour,
   While the rope coils round and round
Like a serpent at his feet,
And again, in swift retreat,
   Nearly lifts him from the ground.

Then within a prison-yard,
Faces fixed, and stern, and hard,
   Laughter and indecent mirth ;
Ah ! it is the gallows-tree !

Breath of Christian charity,
  Blow, and sweep it from the earth !

Then a school-boy, with his kite
Gleaming in a sky of light,
  And an eager, upward look ;
Steeds pursued through lane and field ;
Fowlers with their snares concealed ;
  And an angler by a brook.

Ships rejoicing in the breeze
Wrecks that float o'er unknown seas,
  Anchors dragged through faithless sand ;
Sea-fog drifting overhead,
And, with lessening line and lead,
  Sailors feeling for the land.

All these scenes do I behold,
These, and many left untold,
  In that building long and low ;
While the wheel goes round and round,
With a drowsy, dreamy sound,
  And the spinners backward go.

THE DISCOVERER OF THE NORTH CAPE

A LEAF FROM KING ALFRED'S OROSIUS

OTHERE, the old sea-captain,
    Who dwelt in Helgoland,
To King Alfred, the Lover of Truth,
Brought a snow-white walrus-tooth,
    Which he held in his brown right hand.

His figure was tall and stately,
    Like a boy's his eye appeared ;
His hair was yellow as hay,
But threads of a silvery gray
    Gleamed in his tawny beard.

Hearty and hale was Othere,
    His cheek had the color of oak ;
With a kind of a laugh in his speech,
Like the sea-tide on a beach,
    As unto the King he spoke.

And Alfred, King of the Saxons,
    Had a book upon his knees,
And wrote down the wondrous tale
Of him who was first to sail
    Into the Arctic seas.

"So far I live to the northward,
No man lives north of me;
To the east are wild mountain-chains,
And beyond them meres and plains;
To the westward all is sea.

"So far I live to the northward,
From the harbor of Skeringes-hale,
If you only sailed by day,
With a fair wind all the way,
More than a month would you sail.

"I own six hundred reindeer,
With sheep and swine beside;
I have tribute from the Finns,
Whalebone and reindeer-skins,
And ropes of walrus-hide.

"I ploughed the land with horses,
But my heart was ill at ease,
For the old seafaring men
Came to me now and then,
With their sagas of the seas; —

"Of Iceland and of Greenland,
And the stormy Hebrides,
And the undiscovered deep; —
Oh I could not eat nor sleep
For thinking of those seas.

"To the northward stretched the desert
　　How far I fain would know;
So at last I sallied forth,
And three days sailed due north,
　　As far as the whale-ships go.

"To the west of me was the ocean,
　　To the right the desolate shore,
But I did not slacken sail
For the walrus or the whale,
　　Till after three days more.

"The days grew longer and longer,
　　Till they became as one,
And northward through the haze
I saw the sullen blaze
　　Of the red midnight sun.

"And then uprose before me,
　　Upon the water's edge,
The huge and haggard shape
Of that unknown North Cape,
　　Whose form is like a wedge.

"The sea was rough and stormy,
　　The tempest howled and wailed,
And the sea-fog, like a ghost,
Haunted that dreary coast,
　　But onward still I sailed.

211

"Four days I steered to eastward,
  Four days without a night :
Round in a fiery ring
Went the great sun, O King,
  With red and lurid light."

Here Alfred, King of the Saxons,
  Ceased writing for a while ;
And raised his eyes from his book,
With a strange and puzzled look,
  And an incredulous smile.

But Othere, the old sea-captain,
  He neither paused nor stirred,
Till the King listened, and then
Once more took up his pen,
  And wrote down every word.

"And now the land," said Othere,
  "Bent southward suddenly,
And I followed the curving shore
And ever southward bore
  Into a nameless sea.

"And there we hunted the walrus,
  The narwhale, and the seal ;
Ha ! 't was a noble game !
And like the lightning's flame
  Flew our harpoons of steel.

"There were six of us all together,
    Norsemen of Helgoland ;
In two days and no more
We killed of them threescore,
    And dragged them to the strand ! "

Here Alfred the Truth-teller
    Suddenly closed his book,
And lifted his blue eyes,
With doubt and strange surmise
    Depicted in their look.

And Othere the old sea-captain
    Stared at him wild and weird,
Then smiled, till his shining teeth
Gleamed white from underneath
    His tawny, quivering beard.

And to the King of the Saxons,
    In witness of the truth,
Raising his noble head,
He stretched his brown hand, and said,
    "Behold this walrus-tooth ! "

THE FIFTIETH BIRTHDAY OF AGASSIZ

MAY 28, 1857

IT was fifty years ago
    In the pleasant month of May,
In the beautiful Pays de Vaud,
    A child in its cradle lay.

And Nature, the old nurse, took
    The child upon her knee,
Saying : '' Here is a story-book
    Thy Father has written for thee.''

''Come, wander with me,'' she said,
    '' Into regions yet untrod ;
And read what is still unread
    In the manuscripts of God.''

And he wandered away and away
    With Nature, the dear old nurse,
Who sang to him night and day
    The rhymes of the universe.

And whenever the way seemed long,
    Or his heart began to fail,
She would sing a more wonderful song,
    Or tell a more marvellous tale.

So she keeps him still a child,
    And will not let him go,
Though at times his heart beats wild
    For the beautiful Pays de Vaud ;

Though at times he hears in his dreams
    The Ranz des Vaches of old,
And the rush of mountain streams
    From glaciers clear and cold ;

And the mother at home says, " Hark !
    For his voice I listen and yearn ;
It is growing late and dark,
    And my boy does not return ! "

DAYBREAK

A WIND came up out of the sea,
And said, "O mists, make room for me."

It hailed the ships, and cried, "Sail on,
Ye mariners, the night is gone."

And hurried landward far away,
Crying, "Awake! it is the day."

It said unto the forest, "Shout!
Hang all your leafy banners out!"

It touched the wood-bird's folded wing,
And said, "O bird, awake and sing."

And o'er the farms, "O chanticleer,
Your clarion blow; the day is near."

It whispered to the fields of corn,
"Bow down, and hail the coming morn."

It shouted through the belfry-tower,
"Awake, O bell! proclaim the hour."

It crossed the churchyard with a sigh,
And said, "Not yet! in quiet lie."

SANDALPHON

Have you read in the Talmud of old,
In the Legends the Rabbins have told
    Of the limitless realms of the air,
Have you read it, — the marvellous story
Of Sandalphon, the Angel of Glory,
    Sandalphon, the Angel of Prayer?

How, erect, at the outermost gates
Of the City Celestial he waits,
    With his feet on the ladder of light,
That, crowded with angels unnumbered,
By Jacob was seen, as he slumbered
    Alone in the desert at night?

The Angels of Wind and of Fire
Chant only one hymn, and expire
    With the song's irresistible stress ;
Expire in their rapture and wonder,
As harp-strings are broken asunder
    By music they throb to express.

But serene in the rapturous throng,
Unmoved by the rush of the song,
    With eyes unimpassioned and slow,

Among the dead angels, the deathless
Sandalphon stands listening breathless
   To sounds that ascend from below ; —

From the spirits on earth that adore,
From the souls that entreat and implore
   In the fervor and passion of prayer ;
From the hearts that are broken with losses,
And weary with dragging the crosses
   Too heavy for mortals to bear.

And he gathers the prayers as he stands,
And they change into flowers in his hands,
   Into garlands of purple and red ;
And beneath the great arch of the portal,
Through the streets of the City Immortal
   Is wafted the fragrance they shed.

It is but a legend, I know, —
A fable, a phantom, a show,
   Of the ancient Rabbinical lore ;
Yet the old mediæval tradition,
The beautiful, strange superstition,
   But haunts me and holds me the more.

When I look from my window at night,
And the welkin above is all white,
   All throbbing and panting with stars,
Among them majestic is standing

Sandalphon the angel, expanding
  His pinions in nebulous bars.

And the legend, I feel, is a part
Of the hunger and thirst of the heart,
  The frenzy and fire of the brain,
That grasps at the fruitage forbidden,
The golden pomegranates of Eden,
  To quiet its fever and pain.

THE CHILDREN'S HOUR

BETWEEN the dark and the daylight,
   When the night is beginning to lower,
Comes a pause in the day's occupations,
   That is known as the Children's Hour.

I hear in the chamber above me
   The patter of little feet,
The sound of a door that is opened,
   And voices soft and sweet.

From my study I see in the lamplight,
   Descending the broad hall stair
Grave Alice, and laughing Allegra,
   And Edith with golden hair.

A whisper, and then a silence :
   Yet I know by their merry eyes
They are plotting and planning together
   To take me by surprise.

A sudden rush from the stairway,
   A sudden raid from the hall !
By three doors left unguarded
   They enter my castle wall !

THE CHILDREN'S HOUR

They climb up into my turret
    O'er the arms and back of my chair ;
If I try to escape, they surround me ;
    They seem to be everywhere.

They almost devour me with kisses,
    Their arms about me entwine,
Till I think of the Bishop of Bingen
    In his Mouse-Tower on the Rhine !

Do you think, O blue-eyed banditti,
    Because you have scaled the wall,
Such an old mustache as I am
    Is not a match for you all !

I have you fast in my fortress,
    And will not let you depart,
But put you down into the dungeon
    In the round-tower of my heart.

And there will I keep you forever,
    Yes, forever and a day,
Till the walls shall crumble to ruin,
    And moulder in dust away !

ENCELADUS

Under Mount Etna he lies,
    It is slumber, it is not death ;
For he struggles at times to arise,
And above him the lurid skies
    Are hot with his fiery breath.

The crags are piled on his breast,
    The earth is heaped on his head ;
But the groans of his wild unrest,
Though smothered and half suppressed,
    Are heard, and he is not dead.

And the nations far away
    Are watching with eager eyes ;
They talk together and say,
" To-morrow, perhaps to-day,
    Enceladus will arise ! "

And the old gods, the austere
    Oppressors in their strength
Stand aghast and white with fear
At the ominous sounds they hear,
    And tremble, and mutter, " At length ! "

Ah me ! for the land that is sown
　With the harvest of despair !
Where the burning cinders, blown
From the lips of the overthrown
　Enceladus, fill the air ;

Where ashes are heaped in drifts
　Over vineyard and field and town,
Whenever he starts and lifts
His head through the blackened rifts
　Of the crags that keep him down.

See, see ! the red light shines !
　'T is the glare of his awful eyes !
And the storm-wind shouts through the pines
Of Alps and of Apennines,
　" Enceladus, arise ! "

THE CUMBERLAND

At anchor in Hampton Roads we lay,
   On board of the Cumberland, sloop-of-war ;
And at times from the fortress across the bay
     The alarum of drums swept past,
     Or a bugle blast
   From the camp on the shore.

Then far away to the south uprose
   A little feather of snow-white smoke,
And we knew that the iron ship of our foes
     Was steadily steering its course
     To try the force
   Of our ribs of oak.

Down upon us heavily runs,
   Silent and sullen, the floating fort ;
Then comes a puff of smoke from her guns,
     And leaps the terrible death,
     With fiery breath,
   From each open port.

We are not idle, but send her straight
   Defiance back in a full broadside !
As hail rebounds from a roof of slate,
     Rebounds our heavier hail
     From each iron scale
   Of the monster's hide.

"Strike your flag!" the rebel cries,
    In his arrogant old plantation strain.
"Never!" our gallant Morris replies;
        "It is better to sink than to yield!"
        And the whole air pealed
    With the cheers of our men.

Then, like a kraken huge and black,
    She crushed our ribs in her iron grasp!
Down went the Cumberland all a wrack,
        With a sudden shudder of death,
        And the cannon's breath
    For her dying gasp.

Next morn, as the sun rose over the bay,
    Still floated our flag at the mainmast head.
Lord, how beautiful was Thy day!
        Every waft of the air
        Was a whisper of prayer,
    Or a dirge for the dead.

Ho! brave hearts that went down in the seas!
    Ye are at peace in the troubled stream;
Ho! brave land! with hearts like these,
        Thy flag, that is rent in twain,
        Shall be one again,
    And without a seam!

SNOW–FLAKES

Out of the bosom of the Air,
   Out of the cloud-folds of her garments shaken,
Over the woodlands brown and bare,
   Over the harvest-fields forsaken,
     Silent, and soft, and slow
     Descends the snow.

Even as our cloudy fancies take
   Suddenly shape in some divine expression,
Even as the troubled heart doth make
   In the white countenance confession,
     The troubled sky reveals
     The grief it feels.

This is the poëm of the air,
   Slowly in silent syllables recorded ;
This is the secret of despair,
   Long in its cloudy bosom hoarded,
     Now whispered and revealed
     To wood and field.

A DAY OF SUNSHINE

O GIFT of God ! O perfect day :
Whereon shall no man work, but play ;
Whereon it is enough for me,
Not to be doing, but to be !

Through every fibre of my brain,
Through every nerve, through every vein,
I feel the electric thrill, the touch
Of life, that seems almost too much.

I hear the wind among the trees
Playing celestial symphonies ;
I see the branches downward bent,
Like keys of some great instrument.

And over me unrolls on high
The splendid scenery of the sky,
Where through a sapphire sea the sun
Sails like a golden galleon,

Towards yonder cloud-land in the West
Towards yonder Islands of the Blest,
Whose steep sierra far uplifts
Its craggy summits white with drifts.

Blow, winds ! and waft through all the rooms
The snow-flakes of the cherry-blooms !
Blow, winds ! and bend within my reach
The fiery blossoms of the peach !

O Life and Love ! O happy throng
Of thoughts, whose only speech is song !
O heart of man ! canst thou not be
Blithe as the air is, and as free ?

SOMETHING LEFT UNDONE

Labor with what zeal we will,
  Something still remains undone,
Something uncompleted still
  Waits the rising of the sun.

By the bedside, on the stair,
  At the threshold, near the gates,
With its menace or its prayer,
  Like a mendicant it waits ;

Waits, and will not go away ;
  Waits, and will not be gainsaid ;
By the cares of yesterday
  Each to-day is heavier made ;

Till at length the burden seems
  Greater than our strength can bear,
Heavy as the weight of dreams,
  Pressing on us everywhere.

And we stand from day to day,
  Like the dwarfs of times gone by,
Who, as Northern legends say,
  On their shoulders held the sky.

CHRISTMAS BELLS

I HEARD the bells on Christmas Day
Their old, familiar carols play,
 And wild and sweet
 The words repeat
Of peace on earth, good-will to men !

And thought how, as the day had come,
The belfries of all Christendom
 Had rolled along
 The unbroken song
Of peace on earth, good-will to men !

Till, ringing, singing on its way,
The world revolved from night to day,
 A voice, a chime,
 A chant sublime
Of peace on earth, good-will to men !

Then from each black, accursed mouth
The cannon thundered in the South,
 And with the sound
 The carols drowned
Of peace on earth, good-will to men !

It was as if an earthquake rent
The hearth-stones of a continent,
 And made forlorn
 The households born
Of peace on earth, good-will to men !

And in despair I bowed my head ;
" There is no peace on earth," I said ;
 " For hate is strong,
 And mocks the song
Of peace on earth, good-will to men ! "

Then pealed the bells more loud and deep
" God is not dead ; nor doth he sleep !
 The Wrong shall fail,
 The Right prevail,
With peace on earth, good-will to men ! "

THE CASTLE–BUILDER

A GENTLE boy, with soft and silken locks,
   A dreamy boy, with brown and tender eyes,
A castle-builder, with his wooden blocks,
   And towers that touch imaginary skies.

A fearless rider on his father's knee
   An eager listener unto stories told
At the Round Table of the nursery,
   Of heroes and adventures manifold.

There will be other towers for thee to build ;
   There will be other steeds for thee to ride ;
There will be other legends, and all filled
   With greater marvels and more glorified.

Build on, and make thy castles high and fair,
   Rising and reaching upward to the skies ;
Listening to voices in the upper air,
   Nor lose thy simple faith in mysteries.

A castle-builder, with his wooden blocks,
And towers that touch imaginary skies

Olive ush

THE BROOK AND THE WAVE

THE brooklet came from the mountain,
  As sang the bard of old,
Running with feet of silver
  Over the sands of gold !

Far away in the briny ocean
  There rolled a turbulent wave,
Now singing along the sea-beach,
  Now howling along the cave.

And the brooklet has found the billow,
  Though they flowed so far apart,
And has filled with its freshness and sweetness
  That turbulent, bitter heart !

THE OLD BRIDGE AT FLORENCE

Taddeo Gaddi built me. I am old,
    Five centuries old. I plant my foot of stone
    Upon the Arno, as St. Michael's own
    Was planted on the dragon. Fold by fold
Beneath me as it struggles, I behold
    Its glistening scales. Twice hath it overthrown
    My kindred and companions. Me alone
    It moveth not, but is by me controlled.
I can remember when the Medici
    Were driven from Florence ; longer still ago
    The final wars of Ghibelline and Guelf.
Florence adorns me with her jewelry ;
    And when I think that Michael Angelo
    Hath leaned on me, I glory in myself.

TRAVELS BY THE FIRESIDE

THE ceaseless rain is falling fast,
　　And yonder gilded vane,
Immovable for three days past,
　　Points to the misty main.

It drives me in upon myself
　　And to the fireside gleams,
To pleasant books that crowd my shelf,
　　And still more pleasant dreams.

I read whatever bards have sung
　　Of lands beyond the sea,
And the bright days when I was young
　　Come thronging back to me.

I fancy I can hear again
　　The Alpine torrent's roar,
The mule-bells on the hills of Spain,
　　The sea at Elsinore.

I see the convent's gleaming wall
　　Rise from its groves of pine,
And towers of old cathedrals tall,
　　And castles by the Rhine.

TRAVELS BY THE FIRESIDE

I journey on by park and spire,
    Beneath centennial trees,
Through fields with poppies all on fire
    And gleams of distant seas.

I fear no more the dust and heat,
    No more I feel fatigue,
While journeying with another's feet
    O'er many a lengthening league.

Let others traverse sea and land,
    And toil through various climes,
I turn the world round with my hand
    Reading these poets' rhymes.

From them I learn whatever lies
    Beneath each changing zone,
And see, when looking with their eyes,
    Better than with mine own.

THE SERMON OF ST. FRANCIS

Up soared the lark into the air,
A shaft of song, a wingèd prayer,
As if a soul released from pain
Were flying back to heaven again.

St. Francis heard : it was to him
An emblem of the Seraphim ;
The upward motion of the fire,
The light, the heat, the heart's desire.

Around Assisi's convent gate
The birds, God's poor who cannot wait,
From moor and mere and darksome wood
Come flocking for their dole of food.

" O brother birds," St. Francis said,
" Ye come to me and ask for bread,
But not with bread alone to-day
Shall ye be fed and sent away.

" Ye shall be fed, ye happy birds,
With manna of celestial words ;
Not mine, though mine they seem to be,
Not mine, though they be spoken through me.

" Oh, doubly are ye bound to praise
The great Creator in your lays ;
He giveth you your plumes of down,
Your crimson hoods, your cloaks of brown.

" He giveth you your wings to fly
And breathe a purer air on high,
And careth for you everywhere,
Who for yourselves so little care ! "

With flutter of swift wings and songs
Together rose the feathered throngs,
And singing scattered far apart ;
Deep peace was in St. Francis' heart.

He knew not if the brotherhood
His homily had understood ;
He only knew that to one ear
The meaning of his words was clear.

SONGO RIVER

Nowhere such a devious stream,
Save in fancy or in dream,
Winding slow through bush and brake,
Links together lake and lake.

Walled with woods or sandy shelf,
Ever doubling on itself
Flows the stream, so still and slow
That it hardly seems to flow.

Never errant knight of old,
Lost in woodland or on wold,
Such a winding path pursued
Through the sylvan solitude.

Never school-boy, in his quest
After hazel-nut or nest,
Through the forest in and out
Wandered loitering thus about.

In the mirror of its tide
Tangled thickets on each side
Hang inverted, and between
Floating cloud or sky serene.

Swift or swallow on the wing
Seems the only living thing,
Or the loon, that laughs and flies
Down to those reflected skies.

Silent stream ! thy Indian name
Unfamiliar is to fame ;
For thou hidest here alone,
Well content to be unknown.

But thy tranquil waters teach
Wisdom deep as human speech,
Moving without haste or noise
In unbroken equipoise.

Though thou turnest no busy mill,
And art ever calm and still,
Even thy silence seems to say
To the traveller on his way : —

" Traveller, hurrying from the heat
Of the city, stay thy feet !
Rest awhile, nor longer waste
Life with inconsiderate haste !

" Be not like a stream that brawls
Loud with shallow waterfalls,
But in quiet self-control
Link together soul and soul."

A DUTCH PICTURE

Simon Danz has come home again,
   From cruising about with his buccaneers ;
He has singed the beard of the King of Spain,
And carried away the Dean of Jaen
   And sold him in Algiers.

In his house by the Maese, with its roof of tiles,
   And weathercocks flying aloft in air,
There are silver tankards of antique styles,
Plunder of convent and castle, and piles
   Of carpets rich and rare.

In his tulip-garden there by the town,
   Overlooking the sluggish stream,
With his Moorish cap and dressing-gown,
The old sea-captain, hale and brown,
   Walks in a waking dream.

A smile in his gray mustachio lurks
   Whenever he thinks of the King of Spain,
And the listed tulips look like Turks,
And the silent gardener as he works
   Is changed to the Dean of Jaen.

A DUTCH PICTURE

The windmills on the outermost
   Verge of the landscape in the haze,
To him are towers on the Spanish coast,
With whiskered sentinels at their post,
   Though this is the river Maese.

But when the winter rains begin,
   He sits and smokes by the blazing brands,
And old seafaring men come in,
Goat-bearded, gray, and with double chin,
   And rings upon their hands.

They sit there in the shadow and shine
   Of the flickering fire of the winter night ;
Figures in color and design
Like those by Rembrandt of the Rhine,
   Half darkness and half light.

And they talk of ventures lost or won,
   And their talk is ever and ever the same,
While they drink the red wine of Tarragon,
From the cellars of some Spanish Don,
   Or convent set on flame.

Restless at times with heavy strides
   He paces his parlor to and fro ;
He is like a ship that at anchor rides,
And swings with the rising and falling tides,
   And tugs at her anchor-tow.

Voices mysterious far and near,
  Sound of the wind and sound of the sea,
Are calling and whispering in his ear,
" Simon Danz ! Why stayest thou here ?
  Come forth and follow me ! "

So he thinks he shall take to the sea again
  For one more cruise with his buccaneers,
To singe the beard of the King of Spain,
And capture another Dean of Jaen
  And sell him in Algiers.

CASTLES IN SPAIN

How much of my young heart, O Spain,
   Went out to thee in days of yore !
What dreams romantic filled my brain,
And summoned back to life again
The Paladins of Charlemagne,
   The Cid Campeador !

And shapes more shadowy than these,
   In the dim twilight half revealed ;
Phœnician galleys on the seas,
The Roman camps like hives of bees,
The Goth uplifting from his knees
   Pelayo on his shield.

It was these memories perchance,
   From annals of remotest eld,
That lent the colors of romance
To every trivial circumstance,
And changed the form and countenance
   Of all that I beheld.

Old towns, whose history lies hid
   In monkish chronicle or rhyme, —
Burgos, the birthplace of the Cid,

Zamora and Valladolid,
Toledo, built and walled amid
 The wars of Wamba's time ;

The long, straight line of the highway
 The distant town that seems so near,
The peasants in the fields, that stay
Their toil to cross themselves and pray,
When from the belfry at midday
 The Angelus they hear ;

White crosses in the mountain pass,
 Mules gay with tassels, the loud din
Of muleteers, the tethered ass
That crops the dusty wayside grass,
And cavaliers with spurs of brass
 Alighting at the inn ;

White hamlets hidden in fields of wheat,
 White cities slumbering by the sea,
White sunshine flooding square and street,
Dark mountain ranges, at whose feet
The river beds are dry with heat, —
 All was a dream to me.

Yet something sombre and severe
 O'er the enchanted landscape reigned ;
A terror in the atmosphere
As if King Philip listened near,

Or Torquemada, the austere,
　His ghostly sway maintained.

The softer Andalusian skies
　Dispelled the sadness and the gloom ;
There Cadiz by the seaside lies,
And Seville's orange-orchards rise,
Making the land a paradise
　Of beauty and of bloom.

There Cordova is hidden among
　The palm, the olive, and the vine ;
Gem of the South, by poets sung,
And in whose mosque Almanzor hung
As lamps the bells that once had rung
　At Compostella's shrine.

But over all the rest supreme
　The star of stars, the cynosure,
The artist's and the poet's theme
The young man's vision, the old man's dream, —
Granada by its winding stream,
　The city of the Moor !

And there the Alhambra still recalls
　Aladdin's palace of delight :
Allah il Allah ! through its halls
Whispers the fountain as it falls,
The Darro darts beneath its walls,
　The hills with snow are white.

Ah yes, the hills are white with snow,
  And cold with blasts that bite and freeze ;
But in the happy vale below
The orange and pomegranate grow,
And wafts of air toss to and fro,
  The blossoming almond trees.

The Vega cleft by the Xenil,
  The fascination and allure
Of the sweet landscape chains the will ;
The traveller lingers on the hill,
His parted lips are breathing still
  The last sigh of the Moor.

How like a ruin overgrown
  With flowers that hide the rents of time,
Stands now the Past that I have known ;
Castles in Spain, not built of stone
But of white summer clouds, and blown
  Into this little mist of rhyme !

THE REVENGE OF RAIN–IN–THE-FACE

In that desolate land and lone,
Where the Big Horn and Yellowstone
   Roar down their mountain path,
By their fires the Sioux Chiefs
Muttered their woes and griefs
   And the menace of their wrath.

" Revenge ! " cried Rain-in-the-Face,
" Revenge upon all the race
   Of the White Chief with yellow hair ! "
And the mountains dark and high
From their crags reëchoed the cry
   Of his anger and despair.

In the meadow, spreading wide
By woodland and river-side
   The Indian village stood ;
All was silent as a dream,
Save the rushing of the stream
   And the blue-jay in the wood.

In his war paint and his beads,
Like a bison among the reeds,
   In ambush the Sitting Bull
Lay with three thousand braves

Crouched in the clefts and caves,
   Savage, unmerciful !

Into the fatal snare
The white Chief with yellow hair
   And his three hundred men
Dashed headlong, sword in hand ;
But of that gallant band
   Not one returned again.

The sudden darkness of death
Overwhelmed them like the breath
   And smoke of a furnace fire
By the river's bank, and between
The rocks of the ravine,
   They lay in their bloody attire.

But the foemen fled in the night,
And Rain-in-the-Face, in his flight,
   Uplifted high in air
As a ghastly trophy, bore
The brave heart, that beat no more
   Of the White Chief with yellow hair.

Whose was the right and the wrong ?
Sing it, O funeral song,
   With a voice that is full of tears,
And say that our broken faith
Wrought all this ruin and scathe,
   In the Year of a Hundred Years.

A BALLAD OF THE FRENCH FLEET

OCTOBER, 1746

Mr. Thomas Prince *loquitur*

A FLEET with flags arrayed
  Sailed from the port of Brest,
And the Admiral's ship displayed
  The signal · "Steer southwest."
For this Admiral D'Anville
  Had sworn by cross and crown
To ravage with fire and steel
  Our helpless Boston Town.

There were rumors in the street,
  In the houses there was fear
Of the coming of the fleet,
  And the danger hovering near.
And while from mouth to mouth
  Spread the tidings of dismay,
I stood in the Old South,
  Saying humbly : "Let us pray !

"O Lord ! we would not advise ;
  But if in thy Providence
A tempest should arise
  To drive the French Fleet hence,

And scatter it far and wide,
  Or sink it in the sea,
We should be satisfied,
  And thine the glory be."

This was the prayer I made,
  For my soul was all on flame,
And even as I prayed
  The answering tempest came ;
It came with a mighty power,
  Shaking the windows and walls,
And tolling the bell in the tower,
  As it tolls at funerals.

The lightning suddenly
  Unsheathed its flaming sword,
And I cried : "Stand still, and see
  The salvation of the Lord ! "
The heavens were black with cloud,
  The sea was white with hail,
And ever more fierce and loud
  Blew the October gale.

The fleet it overtook,
  And the broad sails in the van
Like the tents of Cushan shook,
  Or the curtains of Midian.
Down on the reeling decks
  Crashed the o'erwhelming seas ;

251

Ah, never were there wrecks
  So pitiful as these !

Like a potter's vessel broke
  The great ships of the line ;
They were carried away as a smoke,
  Or sank like lead in the brine.
O Lord ! before thy path
  They vanished and ceased to be,
When thou didst walk in wrath
  With thine horses through the sea !

THE LEAP OF ROUSHAN BEG

MOUNTED on Kyrat strong and fleet,
His chestnut steed with four white feet,
   Roushan Beg, called Kurroglou,
Son of the road and bandit chief,
Seeking refuge and relief,
   Up the mountain pathway flew.

Such was Kyrat's wondrous speed,
Never yet could any steed
   Reach the dust-cloud in his course.
More than maiden, more than wife,
More than gold and next to life
   Roushan the Robber loved his horse.

In the land that lies beyond
Erzeroum and Trebizond,
   Garden-girt his fortress stood ;
Plundered khan, or caravan
Journeying north from Koordistan
   Gave him wealth and wine and food.

Seven hundred and fourscore
Men at arms his livery wore,
   Did his bidding night and day ;

Now, through regions all unknown,
He was wandering, lost, alone,
    Seeking without guide his way.

Suddenly the pathway ends,
Sheer the precipice descends,
    Loud the torrent roars unseen ;
Thirty feet from side to side
Yawns the chasm ; on air must ride
    He who crosses this ravine.

Following close in his pursuit,
At the precipice's foot
    Reyhan the Arab of Orfah
Halted with his hundred men,
Shouting upward from the glen,
    " La Illáh illa Alláh ! "

Gently Roushan Beg caressed
Kyrat's forehead, neck, and breast ;
    Kissed him upon both his eyes,
Sang to him in his wild way,
As upon the topmost spray
    Sings a bird before it flies.

" O my Kyrat, O my steed,
Round and slender as a reed,
    Carry me this peril through !
Satin housings shall be thine,

Shoes of gold, O Kyrat mine,
    O thou soul of Kurroglou !

" Soft thy skin as silken skein,
    Soft as woman's hair thy mane,
        Tender are thine eyes and true ;
    All thy hoofs like ivory shine,
    Polished bright ; O life of mine,
        Leap, and rescue Kurroglou ! "

Kyrat, then, the strong and fleet,
    Drew together his four white feet,
        Paused a moment on the verge,
    Measured with his eye the space,
    And into the air's embrace
        Leaped as leaps the ocean surge.

As the ocean surge o'er sand
    Bears a swimmer safe to land,
        Kyrat safe his rider bore ;
    Rattling down the deep abyss
    Fragments of the precipice
        Rolled like pebbles on a shore.

Roushan's tasselled cap of red
    Trembled not upon his head,
        Careless sat he and upright ;
    Neither hand nor bridle shook,
    Nor his head he turned to look,
        As he galloped out of sight.

Flash of harness in the air,
Seen a moment like the glare
 Of a sword drawn from its sheath ;
Thus the phantom horseman passed,
And the shadow that he cast
 Leaped the cataract underneath.

Reyhan the Arab held his breath
While this vision of life and death
 Passed above him. " Allahu ! "
Cried he. " In all Koordistan
Lives there not so brave a man
 As this Robber Kurroglou ! "

THE THREE KINGS

THREE Kings came riding from far away,
    Melchior and Gaspar and Baltasar ;
Three Wise Men out of the East were they,
And they travelled by night and they slept by day,
    For their guide was a beautiful, wonderful star.

The star was so beautiful, large, and clear,
    That all the other stars of the sky
Became a white mist in the atmosphere,
And by this they knew that the coming was near
    Of the Prince foretold in the prophecy.

Three caskets they bore on their saddle-bows,
    Three caskets of gold with golden keys ;
Their robes were of crimson silk with rows
Of bells and pomegranates and furbelows,
    Their turbans like blossoming almond-trees.

And so the Three Kings rode into the West,
    Through the dusk of night, over hill and dell,
And sometimes they nodded with beard on breast
And sometimes talked, as they paused to rest
    With the people they met at some wayside well.

"Of the child that is born," said Baltasar,
    "Good people, I pray you, tell us the news ;

For we in the East have seen his star,
And have ridden fast, and have ridden far,
   To find and worship the King of the Jews."

And the people answered, " You ask in vain ;
   We know of no king but Herod the Great ! "
They thought the Wise Men were men insane,
As they spurred their horses across the plain,
   Like riders in haste, and who cannot wait.

And when they came to Jerusalem,
   Herod the Great, who had heard this thing,
Sent for the Wise Men and questioned them ;
And said, " Go down unto Bethlehem,
   And bring me tidings of this new king."

So they rode away ; and the star stood still,
   The only one in the gray of morn ;
Yes, it stopped,—it stood still of its own free will,
Right over Bethlehem on the hill,
   The city of David, where Christ was born.

And the Three Kings rode through the gate and the
      guard,
   Through the silent street, till their horses turned
And neighed as they entered the great inn-yard;
But the windows were closed, and the doors were
      barred,
   And only a light in the stable burned.

And cradled there in the scented hay,
   In the air made sweet by the breath of kine,
The little child in the manger lay,
The child, that would be king one day
   Of a kingdom not human but divine.

His mother Mary of Nazareth
   Sat watching beside his place of rest,
Watching the even flow of his breath,
For the joy of life and the terror of death
   Were mingled together in her breast.

They laid their offerings at his feet :
   The gold was their tribute to a King,
The frankincense, with its odor sweet,
Was for the Priest, the Paraclete,
   The myrrh for the body's burying.

And the mother wondered and bowed her head,
   And sat as still as a statue of stone ;
Her heart was troubled yet comforted,
Remembering what the Angel had said
   Of an endless reign and of David's throne.

Then the Kings rode out of the city gate,
   With a clatter of hoofs in proud array ;
But they went not back to Herod the Great,
For they knew his malice and feared his hate,
   And returned to their homes by another way.

THE WHITE CZAR

Dost thou see on the rampart's height
That wreath of mist, in the light
Of the midnight moon? Oh, hist!
It is not a wreath of mist;
It is the Czar, the White Czar,
 Batyushka! Gosudar!

He has heard, among the dead,
The artillery roll o'erhead;
The drums and the tramp of feet
Of his soldiery in the street;
He is awake! the White Czar,
 Batyushka! Gosudar!

He has heard in the grave the cries
Of his people: " Awake! arise! "
He has rent the gold brocade
Whereof his shroud was made;
He is risen! the White Czar,
 Batyushka! Gosudar!

From the Volga and the Don
He has led his armies on,
Over river and morass,
Over desert and mountain pass;
The Czar, the Orthodox Czar,
 Batyushka! Gosudar!

FROM MY ARM-CHAIR

TO THE CHILDREN OF CAMBRIDGE

WHO PRESENTED TO ME, ON MY SEVENTY-SECOND
BIRTHDAY, FEBRUARY 27, 1879, THIS CHAIR MADE
FROM THE WOOD OF THE VILLAGE BLACKSMITH'S
CHESTNUT TREE.

> Mr. Longfellow had this poem, which he wrote on the
> same day, printed on a sheet, and was accustomed to give
> a copy to each child who visited him and sat in the chair.

AM I a king, that I should call my own
　　This splendid ebon throne?
Or by what reason, or what right divine,
　　Can I proclaim it mine?

Only, perhaps, by right divine of song
　　It may to me belong;
Only because the spreading chestnut tree
　　Of old was sung by me.

Well I remember it in all its prime,
　　When in the summer-time
The affluent foliage of its branches made
　　A cavern of cool shade.

There, by the blacksmith's forge, beside the street,
　　Its blossoms white and sweet
Enticed the bees, until it seemed alive,
　　And murmured like a hive.

FROM MY ARM-CHAIR

And when the winds of autumn, with a shout,
    Tossed its great arms about,
The shining chestnuts, bursting from the sheath,
    Dropped to the ground beneath.

And now some fragments of its branches bare,
    Shaped as a stately chair,
Have by my hearthstone found a home at last,
    And whisper of the past.

The Danish king could not in all his pride
    Repel the ocean tide
But, seated in this chair, I can in rhyme
    Roll back the tide of Time.

I see again, as one in vision sees,
    The blossoms and the bees,
And hear the children's voices shout and call,
    And the brown chestnuts fall.

I see the smithy with its fires aglow,
    I hear the bellows blow,
And the shrill hammers on the anvil beat
    The iron white with heat!

And thus, dear children, have ye made for me
    This day a jubilee,
And to my more than threescore years and ten
    Brought back my youth again.

FROM MY ARM-CHAIR

The heart hath its own memory, like the mind,
    And in it are enshrined
The precious keepsakes, into which is wrought
    The giver's loving thought.

Only your love and your remembrance could
    Give life to this dead wood,
And make these branches, leafless now so long
    Blossom again in song.

ROBERT BURNS

I SEE amid the fields of Ayr
A ploughman, who, in foul and fair,
  Sings at his task
So clear, we know not if it is
The laverock's song we hear, or his,
  Nor care to ask.

For him the ploughing of those fields
A more ethereal harvest yields
  Than sheaves of grain;
Songs flush with purple bloom the rye,
The plover's call, the curlew's cry,
  Sing in his brain.

Touched by his hand, the wayside weed
Becomes a flower; the lowliest reed
  Beside the stream
Is clothed with beauty; gorse and grass
And heather, where his footsteps pass,
  The brighter seem.

He sings of love, whose flame illumes
The darkness of lone cottage rooms;
  He feels the force,

264

The treacherous undertow and stress
Of wayward passions, and no less
　　The keen remorse.

At moments, wrestling with his fate,
His voice is harsh, but not with hate;
　　The brush-wood, hung
Above the tavern door, lets fall
Its bitter leaf, its drop of gall
　　Upon his tongue.

But still the music of his song
Rises o'er all, elate and strong ;
　　Its master-chords
Are Manhood, Freedom, Brotherhood,
Its discords but an interlude
　　Between the words.

And then to die so young and leave
Unfinished what he might achieve !
　　Yet better sure
Is this, than wandering up and down,
An old man in a country town,
　　Infirm and poor.

For now he haunts his native land
As an immortal youth; his hand
　　Guides every plough ;
He sits beside each ingle-nook,

His voice is in each rushing brook,
    Each rustling bough.

His presence haunts this room to-night,
A form of mingled mist and light
    From that far coast.
Welcome beneath this roof of mine!
Welcome! this vacant chair is thine,
    Dear guest and ghost!

THE WINDMILL

BEHOLD ! a giant am I!
　　Aloft here in my tower,
　　With my granite jaws I devour
The maize, and the wheat, and the rye,
　　And grind them into flour.

I look down over the farms;
　　In the fields of grain I see
　　The harvest that is to be,
And I fling to the air my arms,
　　For I know it is all for me.

I hear the sound of flails
　　Far off, from the threshing-floors
　　In barns, with their open doors,
And the wind, the wind in my sails,
　　Louder and louder roars.

I stand here in my place,
　　With my foot on the rock below,
　　And whichever way it may blow,
I meet it face to face
　　As a brave man meets his foe.

THE WINDMILL

And while we wrestle and strive,
My master, the miller, stands
And feeds me with his hands;
For he knows who makes him thrive,
Who makes him lord of lands.

On Sundays I take my rest;
Church-going bells begin
Their low, melodious din ;
I cross my arms on my breast,
And all is peace within.

TO THE AVON

FLOW on, sweet river! like his verse
Who lies beneath this sculptured hearse;
Nor wait beside the churchyard wall
For him who cannot hear thy call.

Thy playmate once; I see him now
A boy with sunshine on his brow,
And hear in Stratford's quiet street
The patter of his little feet,

I see him by thy shallow edge
Wading knee-deep amid the sedge;
And lost in thought, as if thy stream
Were the swift river of a dream.

He wonders whitherward it flows;
And fain would follow where it goes,
To the wide world, that shall erelong
Be filled with his melodious song.

Flow on, fair stream! That dream is o er;
He stands upon another shore;
A vaster river near him flows,
And still he follows where it goes.

MAD RIVER

IN THE WHITE MOUNTAINS

Why dost thou wildly rush and roar
　　Mad River, O Mad River?
Wilt thou not pause and cease to pour
Thy hurrying, headlong waters o'er
　　This rocky shelf forever?

What secret trouble stirs thy breast?
　　Why all this fret and flurry?
Dost thou not know that what is best
In this too restless world is rest
　　From over-work and worry?

THE RIVER

What wouldst thou in these mountains seek,
　　O stranger from the city?
Is it perhaps some foolish freak
Of thine, to put the words I speak
　　Into a plaintive ditty?

TRAVELLER

Yes; I would learn of thee thy song,
　　With all its flowing numbers,

And in a voice as fresh and strong
As thine is, sing it all day long,
   And hear it in my slumbers.

THE RIVER

A brooklet nameless and unknown
   Was I at first, resembling
A little child, that all alone
Comes venturing down the stairs of stone,
   Irresolute and trembling.

Later, by wayward fancies led,
   For the wide world I panted;
Out of the forest, dark and dread,
Across the open fields I fled,
   Like one pursued and haunted.

I tossed my arms, I sang aloud,
   My voice exultant blending
With thunder from the passing cloud,
The wind, the forest bent and bowed,
   The rush of rain descending.

I heard the distant ocean call,
   Imploring and entreating;
Drawn onward, o'er this rocky wall
I plunged, and the loud waterfall
   Made answer to the greeting.

And now, beset with many ills,
 A toilsome life I follow;
Compelled to carry from the hills
These logs to the impatient mills
 Below there in the hollow.

Yet something ever cheers and charms
 The rudeness of my labors;
Daily I water with these arms
The cattle of a hundred farms
 And have the birds for neighbors.

Men call me Mad, and well they may,
 When, full of rage and trouble,
I burst my banks of sand and clay,
And sweep their wooden bridge away,
 Like withered reeds or stubble.

Now go and write thy little rhyme,
 As of thine own creating.
Thou seest the day is past its prime;
I can no longer waste my time;
 The mills are tired of waiting.

DECORATION DAY

SLEEP, comrades, sleep and rest
   On this Field of the Grounded Arms,
Where foes no more molest,
   Nor sentry's shot alarms !

Ye have slept on the ground before,
   And started to your feet
At the cannon's sudden roar,
   Or the drum's redoubling beat.

But in this camp of Death
   No sound your slumber breaks ;
Here is no fevered breath,
   No wound that bleeds and aches.

All is repose and peace,
   Untrampled lies the sod ;
The shouts of battle cease,
   It is the truce of God !

Rest, comrades, rest and sleep !
   The thoughts of men shall be
As sentinels to keep
   Your rest from danger free.

DECORATION DAY

Your silent tents of green
 We deck with fragrant flowers ;
Yours has the suffering been,
 The memory shall be ours.

THE MONK FELIX

FROM "THE GOLDEN LEGEND"

One morning, all alone,
Out of his convent of gray stone,
Into the forest older, darker, grayer,
His lips moving as if in prayer,
His head sunken upon his breast
As in a dream of rest,
Walked the Monk Felix. All about
The broad, sweet sunshine lay without,
Filling the summer air;
And within the woodlands as he trod,
The dusk was like the Truce of God
With worldly woe and care;
Under him lay the golden moss;
And above him the boughs of hoary trees
Waved, and made the sign of the cross,
And whispered their Benedicites;
And from the ground
Rose an odor sweet and fragrant
Of the wild-flowers and the vagrant
Vines that wandered,
Seeking the sunshine, round and round.

These he heeded not, but pondered
On the volume in his hand,

Wherein amazed he read :
" A thousand years in thy sight
Are but as yesterday when it is past,
And as a watch in the night ! ''
And with his eyes downcast
In humility he said ·
" I believe, O Lord,
What is written in thy Word,
But alas ! I do not understand ! ''

And lo ! he heard
The sudden singing of a bird,
A snow-white bird, that from a cloud
Dropped down,
And among the branches brown
Sat singing,
So sweet, and clear, and loud,
It seemed a thousand harp-strings ringing,
And the Monk Felix closed his book,
And long, long,
With rapturous look,
He listened to the song,
And hardly breathed or stirred,
Until he saw, as in a vision,
The land Elysian,
And in the heavenly city heard
Angelic feet
Fall on the golden flagging of the street.
And he would fain

Have caught the wondrous bird,
But strove in vain ;
For it flew away, away,
Far over hill and dell,
And instead of its sweet singing
He heard the convent bell
Suddenly in the silence ringing
For the service of noonday.
And he retraced
His pathway homeward sadly and in haste.

In the convent there was a change !
He looked for each well-known face,
But the faces were new and strange ;
New figures sat in the oaken stalls,
New voices chanted in the choir ;
Yet the place was the same place,
The same dusky walls
Of cold, gray stone,
The same cloisters and belfry and spire.

A stranger and alone
Among that brotherhood
The Monk Felix stood.
"Forty years," said a Friar,
"Have I been Prior
Of this convent in the wood,
But for that space
Never have I beheld thy face ! "

The heart of the Monk Felix fell ·
And he answered, with submissive tone,
" This morning, after the hour of Prime,
I left my cell,
And wandered forth alone,
Listening all the time
To the melodious singing
Of a beautiful white bird,
Until I heard
The bells of the convent ringing
Noon from their noisy towers.
It was as if I dreamed ;
For what to me had seemed
Moments only, had been hours ! "

" Years ! " said a voice close by.
It was an aged monk who spoke,
From a bench of oak
Fastened against the wall ; —
He was the oldest monk of all.
For a whole century
Had he been there,
Serving God in prayer,
The meekest and humblest of his creatures.
He remembered well the features
Of Felix, and he said,
Speaking distinct and slow :
"One hundred years ago,
When I was a novice in this place,

There was here a monk, full of God's grace,
Who bore the name
Of Felix, and this man must be the same."

And straightway
They brought forth to the light of day
A volume old and brown,
A huge tome, bound
In brass and wild-boar's hide,
Wherein were written down
The names of all who had died
In the convent, since it was edified.
And there they found,
Just as the old monk said,
That on a certain day and date,
One hundred years before,
Had gone forth from the convent gate
The Monk Felix, and never more
Had entered that sacred door.
He had been counted among the dead!
And they knew, at last,
That, such had been the power
Of that celestial and immortal song,
A hundred years had passed,
And had not seemed so long
As a single hour !

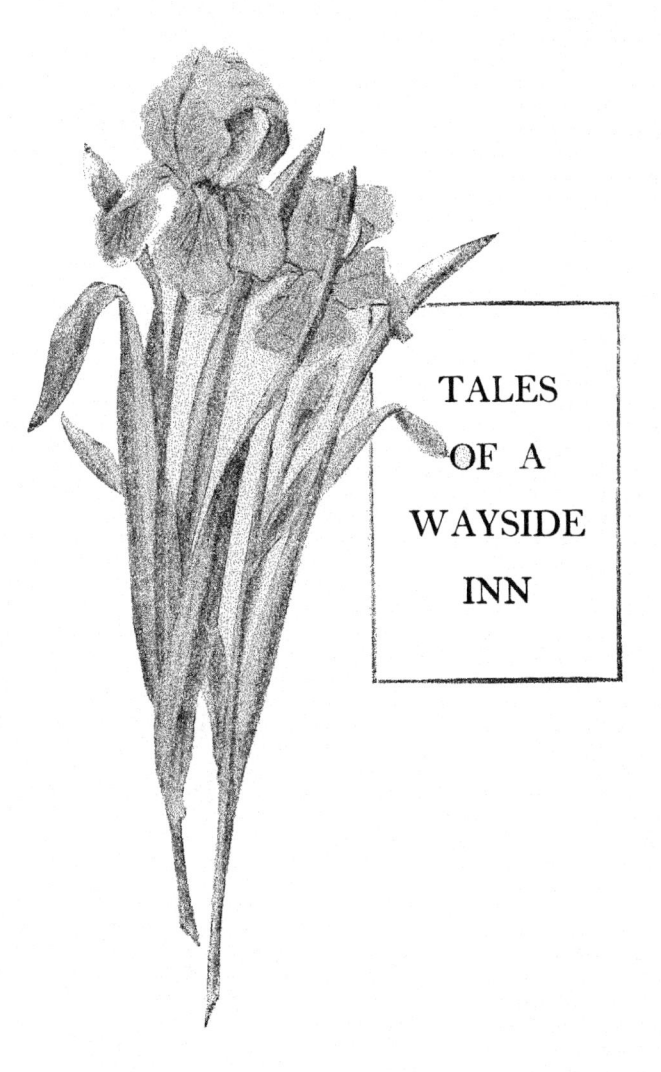

TALES

OF A

WAYSIDE

INN

PAUL REVERE'S RIDE

Listen, my children, and you shall hear
Of the midnight ride of Paul Revere,
On the eighteenth of April, in Seventy-five;
Hardly a man is now alive
Who remembers that famous day and year.

He said to his friend, "If the British march
By land or sea from the town to-night,
Hang a lantern aloft in the belfry-arch
Of the North Church tower as a signal light, —
One, if by land, and two, if by sea;
And I on the opposite shore will be,
Ready to ride and spread the alarm
Through every Middlesex village and farm,
For the country folk to be up and to arm."

Then he said, "Good night!" and with muffled oar
Silently rowed to the Charlestown shore,
Just as the moon rose over the bay,

Where swinging wide at her moorings lay
The Somerset, British man-of-war;
A phantom ship, with each mast and spar
Across the moon like a prison bar,
And a huge black hulk, that was magnified
By its own reflection in the tide.

Meanwhile, his friend, through alley and street,
Wanders and watches with eager ears,
Till in the silence around him he hears
The muster of men at the barrack door,
The sound of arms, and the tramp of feet,
And the measured tread of the grenadiers,
Marching down to their boats on the shore.

Then he climbed the tower of the Old North Church,
By the wooden stairs, with stealthy tread,
To the belfry-chamber overhead,
And startled the pigeons from their perch
On the sombre rafters, that round him made
Masses and moving shapes of shade, —
By the trembling ladder, steep and tall,
To the highest window in the wall,
Where he paused to listen and look down
A moment on the roofs of the town,
And the moonlight flowing over all.

Beneath, in the churchyard, lay the dead,
In their night-encampment on the hill,
Wrapped in silence so deep and still

That he could hear, like a sentinel's tread,
The watchful night-wind, as it went
Creeping along from tent to tent,
And seeming to whisper, "All is well!"
A moment only he feels the spell
Of the place and the hour, and the secret dread
Of the lonely belfry and the dead;
For suddenly all his thoughts are bent
On a shadowy something far away,
Where the river widens to meet the bay,—
A line of black that bends and floats
On the rising tide, like a bridge of boats.

Meanwhile, impatient to mount and ride,
Booted and spurred, with a heavy stride
On the opposite shore walked Paul Revere.
Now he patted his horse's side,
Now gazed at the landscape far and near,
Then, impetuous, stamped the earth,
And turned and tightened his saddle-girth;
But mostly he watched with eager search
The belfry-tower of the Old North Church,
As it rose above the graves on the hill,
Lonely and spectral and sombre and still.
And lo! as he looks, on the belfry's height
A glimmer, and then a gleam of light!
He springs to the saddle, the bridle he turns,
But lingers and gazes, till full on his sight,
A second lamp in the belfry burns!

A hurry of hoofs in a village street,
A shape in the moonlight, a bulk in the dark,
And beneath, from the pebbles, in passing, a spark
Struck out by a steed flying fearless and fleet :
That was all ! And yet, through the gloom and the
      light,
The fate of a nation was riding that night ;
And the spark struck out by that steed, in his flight,
Kindled the land into flame with its heat.

He has left the village and mounted the steep,
And beneath him, tranquil and broad and deep,
Is the Mystic, meeting the ocean tides ;
And under the alders that skirt its edge,
Now soft on the sand, now loud on the ledge,
Is heard the tramp of his steed as he rides.

It was twelve by the village clock,
When he crossed the bridge into Medford town.
He heard the crowing of the cock,
And the barking of the farmer's dog,
And felt the damp of the river fog,
That rises after the sun goes down.

It was one by the village clock,
When he galloped into Lexington.
He saw the gilded weathercock
Swim in the moonlight as he passed,
And the meeting-house windows, blank and bare,

A voice in the darkness, a knock at the door

Gaze at him with a spectral glare,
As if they already stood aghast
At the bloody work they would look upon.

It was two by the village clock,
When he came to the bridge in Concord town.
He heard the bleating of the flock,
And the twitter of birds among the trees,
And felt the breath of the morning breeze
Blowing over the meadows brown.
And one was safe and asleep in his bed
Who at the bridge would be first to fall,
Who that day would be lying dead,
Pierced by a British musket-ball.

You know the rest.   In the books you have read,
How the British Regulars fired and fled,—
How the farmers gave them ball for ball,
From behind each fence and farm-yard wall,
Chasing the red-coats down the lane,
Then crossing the fields to emerge again
Under the trees at the turn of the road,
And only pausing to fire and load.

So through the night rode Paul Revere;
And so through the night went his cry of alarm
To every Middlesex village and farm, —
A cry of defiance and not of fear,
A voice in the darkness, a knock at the door,

And a word that shall echo forevermore!
For, borne on the night-wind of the Past,
Through all our history, to the last,
In the hour of darkness and peril and need,
The people will waken and listen to hear
The hurrying hoof-beats of that steed
And the midnight message of Paul Revere.

KING ROBERT OF SICILY

ROBERT of Sicily, brother of Pope Urbane
And Valmond, Emperor of Allemaine,
Apparelled in magnificent attire,
With retinue of many a knight and squire,
On St. John's eve, at vespers, proudly sat
And heard the priests chant the Magnificat.
And as he listened, o'er and o'er again
Repeated, like a burden or refrain,
He caught the words, " *Deposuit potentes*
De sede, et exaltavit humiles ;"
And slowly lifting up his kingly head
He to a learned clerk beside him said,
"What mean these words ? " The clerk made answer
        meet,
" He has put down the mighty from their seat,
And has exalted them of low degree."
Thereat King Robert muttered scornfully,
" 'T is well that such seditious words are sung
Only by priests and in the Latin tongue ;
For unto priests and people be it known,
There is no power can push me from my throne !"
And leaning back, he yawned and fell asleep,
Lulled by the chant monotonous and deep.
When he awoke, it was already night ;

The church was empty, and there was no light,
Save where the lamps, that glimmered few and faint,
Lighted a little space before some saint.
He started from his seat and gazed around,
But saw no living thing and heard no sound.
He groped towards the door, but it was locked;
He cried aloud, and listened, and then knocked,
And uttered awful threatenings and complaints,
And imprecations upon men and saints.
The sounds reëchoed from the roof and walls
As if dead priests were laughing in their stalls.

At length the sexton, hearing from without
The tumult of the knocking and the shout,
And thinking thieves were in the house of prayer,
Came with his lantern, asking, "Who is there?"
Half choked with rage, King Robert fiercely said,
"Open: 't is I, the King! Art thou afraid?"
The frightened sexton, muttering, with a curse,
"This is some drunken vagabond, or worse!"
Turned the great key and flung the portal wide;
A man rushed by him at a single stride,
Haggard, half naked, without hat or cloak,
Who neither turned, nor looked at him, nor spoke,
But leaped into the blackness of the night,
And vanished like a spectre from his sight.

Robert of Sicily, brother of Pope Urbane
And Valmond, Emperor of Allemaine,

Despoiled of his magnificent attire,
Bareheaded, breathless, and besprent with mire,
With sense of wrong and outrage desperate,
Strode on and thundered at the palace gate ;
Rushed through the courtyard, thrusting in his rage
To right and left each seneschal and page,
And hurried up the broad and sounding stair,
His white face ghastly in the torches' glare.
From hall to hall he passed with breathless speed ;
Voices and cries he heard, but did not heed,
Until at last he reached the banquet-room,
Blazing with light, and breathing with perfume.

There on the dais sat another king,
Wearing his robes, his crown, his signet-ring,
King Robert's self in features, form, and height,
But all transfigured with angelic light!
It was an Angel; and his presence there
With a divine effulgence filled the air,
An exaltation, piercing the disguise,
Though none the hidden Angel recognize.

A moment speechless, motionless, amazed,
The throneless monarch on the Angel gazed,
Who met his look of anger and surprise
With the divine compassion of his eyes ;
Then said, "Who art thou? and why com'st thou here?"
To which King Robert answered with a sneer,
"I am the King, and come to claim my own

From an impostor, who usurps my throne!"
And suddenly, at these audacious words,
Up sprang the angry guests, and drew their swords;
The Angel answered, with unruffled brow,
"Nay, not the King, but the King's Jester, thou
Henceforth shalt wear the bells and scalloped cape,
And for thy counsellor shalt lead an ape;
Thou shalt obey my servants when they call,
And wait upon my henchmen in the hall!"

Deaf to King Robert's threats and cries and prayers,
They thrust him from the hall and down the stairs;
A group of tittering pages ran before,
And as they opened wide the folding-door,
His heart failed, for he heard, with strange alarms,
The boisterous laughter of the men-at-arms,
And all the vaulted chamber roar and ring
With the mock plaudits of "Long live the King!"

Next morning, waking with the day's first beam,
He said within himself, "It was a dream!"
But the straw rustled as he turned his head,
There were the cap and bells beside his bed,
Around him rose the bare, discolored walls,
Close by, the steeds were champing in their stalls,
And in the corner, a revolting shape,
Shivering and chattering sat the wretched ape.
It was no dream; the world he loved so much
Had turned to dust and ashes at his touch!

Days came and went ; and now returned again
To Sicily the old Saturnian reign ;
Under the Angel's governance benign
The happy island danced with corn and wine,
And deep within the mountain's burning breast
Enceladus, the giant, was at rest.

Meanwhile King Robert yielded to his fate,
Sullen and silent and disconsolate.
Dressed in the motley garb that Jesters wear,
With look bewildered and a vacant stare,
Close shaven above the ears, as monks are shorn,
By courtiers mocked, by pages laughed to scorn,
His only friend the ape, his only food
What others left,— he still was unsubdued.
And when the Angel met him on his way,
And half in earnest, half in jest, would say,
Sternly, though tenderly, that he might feel
The velvet scabbard held a sword of steel,
" Art thou the King? " the passion of his woe
Burst from him in resistless overflow,
And, lifting high his forehead, he would fling
The haughty answer back, "I am, I am the King ! "

Almost three years were ended ; when there came
Ambassadors of great repute and name
From Valmond, Emperor of Allemaine,
Unto King Robert, saying that Pope Urbane
By letter summoned them forthwith to come

On Holy Thursday to his city of Rome.
The Angel with great joy received his guests,
And gave them presents of embroidered vests,
And velvet mantles with rich ermine lined,
And rings and jewels of the rarest kind.
Then he departed with them o'er the sea
Into the lovely land of Italy,
Whose loveliness was more resplendent made
By the mere passing of that cavalcade,
With plumes, and cloaks, and housings, and the stir
Of jewelled bridle and of golden spur.
And lo! among the menials, in mock state,
Upon a piebald steed, with shambling gait,
His cloak of fox-tails flapping in the wind,
The solemn ape demurely perched behind,
King Robert rode, making huge merriment
In all the country towns through which they went.

The Pope received them with great pomp and blare
Of bannered trumpets, on Saint Peter's square,
Giving his benediction and embrace,
Fervent, and full of apostolic grace.
While with congratulations and with prayers
He entertained the Angel unawares,
Robert, the Jester, bursting through the crowd,
Into their presence rushed, and cried aloud,
"I am the King! Look, and behold in me
Robert, your brother, King of Sicily!
This man, who wears my semblance to your eyes,

Is an impostor in a king's disguise.
Do you not know me? does no voice within
Answer my cry, and say we are akin?"
The Pope in silence, but with troubled mien,
Gazed at the Angel's countenance serene;
The Emperor, laughing, said, "It is strange sport
To keep a madman for thy Fool at court!"
And the poor, baffled Jester in disgrace
Was hustled back among the populace.

In solemn state the Holy Week went by,
And Easter Sunday gleamed upon the sky;
The presence of the Angel, with its light,
Before the sun rose, made the city bright,
And with new fervor filled the hearts of men,
Who felt that Christ indeed had risen again.
Even the Jester, on his bed of straw,
With haggard eyes the unwonted splendor saw,
He felt within a power unfelt before,
And, kneeling humbly on his chamber floor,
He heard the rushing garments of the Lord
Sweep through the silent air, ascending heavenward.

And now the visit ending, and once more
Valmond returning to the Danube's shore,
Homeward the Angel journeyed, and again
The land was made resplendent with his train,
Flashing along the towns of Italy
Unto Salerno, and from thence by sea.

And when once more within Palermo's wall,
And, seated on the throne in his great hall,
He heard the Angelus from convent towers,
As if the better world conversed with ours,
He beckoned to King Robert to draw nigher,
And with a gesture bade the rest retire;
And when they were alone, the Angel said,
"Art thou the King?" Then, bowing down his head,
King Robert crossed both hands upon his breast,
And meekly answered him : "Thou knowest best!
My sins as scarlet are ; let me go hence,
And in some cloister's school of penitence,
Across those stones, that pave the way to heaven,
Walk barefoot, till my guilty soul be shriven!"

The Angel smiled, and from his radiant face
A holy light illumined all the place,
And through the open window, loud and clear,
They heard the monks chant in the chapel near,
Above the stir and tumult of the street :
"He has put down the mighty from their seat,
And has exalted them of low degree!"
And through the chant a second melody
Rose like the throbbing of a single string :
"I am an Angel, and thou art the King!"

King Robert, who was standing near the throne,
Lifted his eyes, and lo! he was alone!

But all apparelled as in days of old,
With ermined mantle and with cloth of gold;
And when his courtiers came, they found him there
Kneeling upon the floor, absorbed in silent prayer.

THE BUILDING OF THE LONG SERPENT

THORBERG SKAFTING, master-builder,
    In his ship-yard by the sea,
Whistling, said, "It would bewilder
Any man but Thorberg Skafting,
    Any man but me!"

Near him lay the Dragon stranded,
    Built of old by Raud the Strong,
And King Olaf had commanded
He should build another Dragon,
    Twice as large and long.

Therefore whistled Thorberg Skafting,
    As he sat with half-closed eyes,
And his head turned sideways, drafting
That new vessel for King Olaf
    Twice the Dragon's size.

Round him busily hewed and hammered
    Mallet huge and heavy axe ;
Workmen laughed and sang and clamored ;
Whirred the wheels, that into rigging
    Spun the shining flax !

" Men shall hear of Thorberg Skafting
For a hundred year !"

All this tumult heard the master, —
　　It was music to his ear ;
Fancy whispered all the faster,
" Men shall hear of Thorberg Skafting
　　For a hundred year! "

Workmen sweating at the forges
　　Fashioned iron bolt and bar,
Like a warlock's midnight orgies
Smoked and bubbled the black caldron
　　With the boiling tar.

Did the warlocks mingle in it
　　Thorberg Skafting, any curse ?
Could you not be gone a minute
But some mischief must be doing,
　　Turning bad to worse ?

Twas an ill wind that came wafting
　　From his homestead words of woe;
To his farm went Thorberg Skafting,
Oft repeating to his workmen,
　　Build ye thus and so.

After long delays returning
　　Came the master back by night;
To his ship-yard longing, yearning,
Hurried he, and did not leave it
　　Till the morning's light.

"Come and see my ship, my darling!"
On the morrow said the King;
"Finished now from keel to carling;
Never yet was seen in Norway
Such a wondrous thing!"

In the ship-yard, idly talking,
At the ship the workmen stared:
Some one, all their labor balking,
Down her sides had cut deep gashes,
Not a plank was spared!

"Death be to the evil-doer!"
With an oath King Olaf spoke!"
"But rewards to his pursuer!"
And with wrath his face grew redder
Than his scarlet cloak.

Straight the master-builder, smiling,
Answered thus the angry King ·
"Cease blaspheming and reviling
Olaf, it was Thorberg Skafting
Who has done this thing!"

Then he chipped and smoothed the planking,
Till the King, delighted, swore,
With much lauding and much thanking,
"Handsomer is now my Dragon
Than she was before!"

Seventy ells and four extended
   On the grass the vessel's keel;
High above it, gilt and splendid,
Rose the figure-head ferocious
   With its crest of steel.

Then they launched her from the tressels,
   In the ship-yard by the sea;
She was the grandest of all vessels,
Never ship was built in Norway
   Half so fine as she!

The Long Serpent was she christened,
   'Mid the roar of cheer on cheer!
They who to the Saga listened
Heard the name of Thorberg Skafting
   For a hundred year!

THE BELL OF ATRI

At Atri in Abruzzo, a small town
Of ancient Roman date, but scant renown,
One of those little places that have run
Half up the hill, beneath a blazing sun,
And then sat down to rest, as if to say,
"I climb no farther upward, come what may," —
The Re Giovanni, now unknown to fame,
So many monarchs since have borne the name,
Had a great bell hung in the market-place,
Beneath a roof, projecting some small space
By way of shelter from the sun and rain.
Then rode he through the streets with all his train,
And, with the blast of trumpets loud and long,
Made proclamation, that whenever wrong
Was done to any man, he should but ring
The great bell in the square, and he, the King,
Would cause the Syndic to decide thereon.
Such was the proclamation of King John.

How swift the happy days in Atri sped,
What wrongs were righted, need not here be said.
Suffice it that, as all things must decay,
The hempen rope at length was worn away,
Unravelled at the end, and, strand by strand,

Loosened and wasted in the ringer's hand
Till one, who noted this in passing by,
Mended the rope with braids of briony,
So that the leaves and tendrils of the vine
Hung like a votive garland at a shrine.

By chance it happened that in Atri dwelt
A knight, with spur on heel and sword in belt,
Who loved to hunt the wild-boar in the woods,
Who loved his falcons with their crimson hoods,
Who loved his hounds and horses, and all sports
And prodigalities of camps and courts ; —
Loved, or had loved them ; for at last, grown old,
His only passion was the love of gold.

He sold his horses, sold his hawks and hounds,
Rented his vineyards and his garden-grounds,
Kept but one steed, his favorite steed of all,
To starve and shiver in a naked stall,
And day by day sat brooding in his chair,
Devising plans how best to hoard and spare.

At length he said · "What is the use or need
To keep at my own cost this lazy steed,
Eating his head off in my stables here,
When rents are low and provender is dear?
Let him go feed upon the public ways ;
I want him only for the holidays."
So the old steed was turned into the heat

Of the long, lonely, silent, shadeless street;
And wandered in suburban lanes forlorn,
Barked at by dogs, and torn by brier and thorn.

One afternoon, as in that sultry clime
It is the custom in the summer time,
With bolted doors and window-shutters closed,
The inhabitants of Atri slept or dozed;
When suddenly upon their senses fell
The loud alarm of the accusing bell!
The Syndic started from his deep repose,
Turned on his couch, and listened, and then rose
And donned his robes, and with reluctant pace
Went panting forth into the market-place,
Where the great bell upon its cross-beams swung,
Reiterating with persistent tongue,
In half-articulate jargon, the old song ·
"Some one hath done a wrong, hath done a wrong!"

But ere he reached the belfry's light arcade
He saw, or thought he saw, beneath its shade,
No shape of human form of woman born,
But a poor steed dejected and forlorn,
Who with uplifted head and eager eye
Was tugging at the vines of briony.
"Domeneddio!" cried the Syndic straight,
"This is the Knight of Atri's steed of state!
He calls for justice, being sore distressed,
And pleads his cause as loudly as the best."

Meanwhile from street and lane a noisy crowd
Had rolled together like a summer cloud,
And told the story of the wretched beast
In five-and-twenty different ways at least,
With much gesticulation and appeal
To heathen gods, in their excessive zeal.
The Knight was called and questioned ; in reply
Did not confess the fact, did not deny ;
Treated the matter as a pleasant jest,
And set at naught the Syndic and the rest,
Maintaining, in an angry undertone,
That he should do what pleased him with his own.

And thereupon the Syndic gravely read
The proclamation of the King; then said:
" Pride goeth forth on horseback grand and gay,
But cometh back on foot, and begs its way;
Fame is the fragrance of heroic deeds,
Of flowers of chivalry and not of weeds !
These are familiar proverbs ; but I fear
They never yet have reached your knightly ear.
What fair renown, what honor, what repute
Can come to you from starving this poor brute ?
He who serves well and speaks not, merits more
Than they who clamor loudest at the door.
Therefore the law decrees that as this steed
Served you in youth, henceforth you shall take heed
To comfort his old age, and to provide
Shelter in stall, and food and field beside."

The Knight withdrew abashed; the people all
Led home the steed in triumph to his stall.
The King heard and approved, and laughed in glee,
And cried aloud: " Right well it pleaseth me !
Church-bells at best but ring us to the door;
But go not into mass ; my bell doth more :
It cometh into court and pleads the cause
Of creatures dumb and unknown to the laws ;
And this shall make, in every Christian clime,
The Bell of Atri famous for all time."

THE BALLAD OF CARMILHAN

I

At Stralsund, by the Baltic Sea,
  Within the sandy bar,
At sunset of a summer's day,
Ready for sea, at anchor lay
  The good ship Valdemar.

The sunbeams danced upon the waves,
  And played along her side ;
And through the cabin windows streamed
In ripples of golden light, that seemed
  The ripple of the tide.

There sat the captain with his friends,
  Old skippers brown and hale,
Who smoked and grumbled o'er their grog,
And talked of iceberg and of fog,
  Of calm and storm and gale.

And one was spinning a sailor's yarn
  About Klaboterman
The Kobold of the sea ; a spright
Invisible to mortal sight,
  Who o'er the rigging ran.

Sometimes he hammered in the hold,
　　Sometimes upon the mast,
Sometimes abeam, sometimes abaft,
Or at the bows he sang and laughed,
　　And made all tight and fast.

He helped the sailors at their work,
　　And toiled with jovial din ;
He helped them hoist and reef the sails,
He helped them stow the casks and bales,
　　And heave the anchor in.

But woe unto the lazy louts,
　　The idlers of the crew ;
Them to torment was his delight,
And worry them by day and night,
　　And pinch them black and blue.

And woe to him whose mortal eyes
　　Klaboterman behold.
It is a certain sign of death ! —
The cabin-boy here held his breath,
　　He felt his blood run cold.

II

The jolly skipper paused awhile,
　　And then again began ;
"There is a Spectre Ship," quoth he,
" A ship of the Dead that sails the sea,
　　And is called the Carmilhan.

"A ghostly ship, with a ghostly crew,
    In tempests she appears;
And before the gale, or against the gale,
She sails without a rag of sail,
    Without a helmsman steers.

"She haunts the Atlantic north and south,
    But mostly the mid-sea,
Where three great rocks rise bleak and bare
Like furnace chimneys in the air,
    And are called the Chimneys Three.

"And ill betide the luckless ship
    That meets the Carmilhan;
Over her decks the seas will leap,
She must go down into the deep,
    And perish mouse and man."

The captain of the Valdemar
    Laughed loud with merry heart.
"I should like to see this ship," said he;
"I should like to find these Chimneys Three
    That are marked down in the chart.

"I have sailed right over the spot," he said,
    "With a good stiff breeze behind,
When the sea was blue, and the sky was clear, —
You can follow my course by these pinholes here, —
    And never a rock could find."

And then he swore a dreadful oath,
  He swore by the Kingdoms Three,
That, should he meet the Carmilhan,
He would run her down, although he ran
  Right into Eternity!

All this, while passing to and fro,
  The cabin-boy had heard;
He lingered at the door to hear,
And drank in all with greedy ear,
  And pondered every word.

He was a simple country lad,
  But of a roving mind.
"Oh, it must be like heaven," thought he,
"Those far-off foreign lands to see,
  And fortune seek and find!"

But in the fo'castle, when he heard
  The mariners blaspheme,
He thought of home, he thought of God
And his mother under the churchyard sod,
  And wished it were a dream.

One friend on board that ship had he;
  'T was the Klaboterman,
Who saw the Bible in his chest,
And made a sign upon his breast,
  All evil things to ban.

III

The cabin windows have grown blank
 As eyeballs of the dead;
No more the glancing sunbeams burn
On the gilt letters of the stern,
 But on the figure-head;

On Valdemar Victorious,
 Who looketh with disdain
To see his image in the tide
Dismembered float from side to side,
 And reunite again.

"It is the wind," those skippers said,
 " That swings the vessel so;
It is the wind; it freshens fast,
'T is time to say farewell at last,
 'T is time for us to go."

They shook the captain by the hand,
 "Good luck! good luck!" they cried;
Each face was like the setting sun,
As, broad and red, they one by one
 Went o'er the vessel's side.

The sun went down, the full moon rose,
 Serene o'er field and flood;
And all the winding creeks and bays
And broad sea-meadows seemed ablaze,
 The sky was red as blood.

The southwest wind blew fresh and fair;
　　As fair as wind could be;
Bound for Odessa, o'er the bar,
With all sail set, the Valdemar
　　Went proudly out to sea.

The lovely moon climbs up the sky
　　As one who walks in dreams ;
A tower of marble in her light,
A wall of black, a wall of white,
　　The stately vessel seems.

Low down upon the sandy coast
　　The lights begin to burn ;
And now, uplifted high in air,
They kindle with a fiercer glare,
　　And now drop far astern.

The dawn appears, the land is gone,
　　The sea is all around ;
Then on each hand low hills of sand
Emerge and form another land ;
　　She steereth through the Sound.

Through Kattegat and Skager-rack
　　She flitteth like a ghost ;
By day and night, by night and day,
She bounds, she flies upon her way
　　Along the English coast.

Cape Finisterre is drawing near,
    Cape Finisterre is past ;
Into the open ocean stream
She floats, the vision of a dream
    Too beautiful to last.

Suns rise and set, and rise, and yet
    There is no land in sight ;
The liquid planets overhead
Burn brighter now the moon is dead,
    And longer stays the night.

IV

And now along the horizon's edge
    Mountains of cloud uprose,
Black as with forests underneath,
Above, their sharp and jagged teeth
    Were white as drifted snows.

Unseen behind them sank the sun,
    But flushed each snowy peak
A little while with rosy light,
That faded slowly from the sight
    As blushes from the cheek.

Black grew the sky, — all black, all black ;
    The clouds were everywhere;
There was a feeling of suspense
In nature, a mysterious sense
    Of terror in the air.

And all on board the Valdemar
  Was still as still could be;
Save when the dismal ship-bell tolled,
As ever and anon she rolled,
  And lurched into the sea.

The captain up and down the deck
  Went striding to and fro;
Now watched the compass at the wheel,
Now lifted up his hand to feel
  Which way the wind might blow.

And now he looked up at the sails,
  And now upon the deep;
In every fibre of his frame
He felt the storm before it came,
  He had no thought of sleep.

Eight bells! and suddenly abaft,
  With a great rush of rain,
Making the ocean white with spume,
In darkness like the day of doom,
  On came the hurricane.

The lightning flashed from cloud to cloud,
  And rent the sky in two;
A jagged flame, a single jet
Of white fire, like a bayonet,
  That pierced the eyeballs through.

Then all around was dark again,
   And blacker than before ;
But in that single flash of light
He had beheld a fearful sight,
   And thought of the oath he swore.

For right ahead lay the Ship of the Dead,
   The ghostly Carmilhan !
Her masts were stripped, her yards were bare,
And on her bowsprit, poised in air,
   Sat the Klaboterman.

Her crew of ghosts was all on deck
   Or clambering up the shrouds;
The boatswain's whistle, the captain's hail
Were like the piping of the gale,
   And thunder in the clouds.

And close behind the Carmilhan
   There rose up from the sea,
As from a foundered ship of stone,
Three bare and splintered masts alone:
   They were the Chimneys Three.

And onward dashed the Valdemar
   And leaped into the dark ;
A denser mist, a colder blast,
A little shudder, and she had passed
   Right through the Phantom Bark.

She cleft in twain the shadowy hulk,
　But cleft it unaware ;
As when, careering to her nest,
The sea-gull severs with her breast
　The unresisting air.

Again the lightning flashed ; again
　They saw the Carmilhan,
Whole as before in hull and spar ;
But now on board of the Valdemar
　Stood the Klaboterman.

And they all knew their doom was sealed ;
　They knew that death was near ;
Some prayed who never prayed before,
And some they wept, and some they swore
　And some were mute with fear.

Then suddenly there came a shock,
　And louder than wind or sea
A cry burst from the crew on deck,
As she dashed and crashed, a hopeless wreck,
　Upon the Chimneys Three.

The storm and night were passed, the light
　To streak the east began ;
The cabin-boy, picked up at sea,
Survived the wreck, and only he,
　To tell of the Carmilhan.

THE LEGEND BEAUTIFUL

"Hadst thou stayed, I must have fled!"
That is what the Vision said.

In his chamber all alone,
Kneeling on the floor of stone,
Prayed the Monk in deep contrition
For his sins of indecision,
Prayed for greater self-denial
In temptation and in trial;
It was noonday by the dial,
And the Monk was all alone.

Suddenly, as if it lightened,
An unwonted splendor brightened
All within him and without him
In that narrow cell of stone;
And he saw the Blessed Vision
Of our Lord, with light Elysian
Like a vesture wrapped about Him,
Like a garment round Him thrown.

Not as crucified and slain,
Not in agonies of pain,
Not with bleeding hands and feet,
Did the Monk his Master see;

But as in the village street,
In the house or harvest-field,
Halt and lame and blind He healed,
When He walked in Galilee.

In an attitude imploring,
Hands upon his bosom crossed,
Wondering, worshipping, adoring,
Knelt the Monk in rapture lost.
Lord, he thought, in heaven that reignest,
Who am I, that thus thou deignest
To reveal thyself to me?
Who am I, that from the centre
Of thy glory thou shouldst enter
This poor cell, my guest to be?

Then amid his exaltation,
Loud the convent bell appalling,
From its belfry calling, calling,
Rang through court and corridor
With persistent iteration
He had never heard before.
It was now the appointed hour
When alike in shine or shower,
Winter's cold or summer's heat,
To the convent portals came
All the blind and halt and lame,
All the beggars of the street,
For their daily dole of food

Dealt them by the brotherhood;
And their almoner was he
Who upon his bended knee,
Rapt in silent ecstasy
Of divinest self-surrender,
Saw the Vision and the Splendor.
Deep distress and hesitation
Mingled with his adoration;
Should he go or should he stay?
Should he leave the poor to wait
Hungry at the convent gate,
Till the Vision passed away?
Should he slight his radiant guest,
Slight this visitant celestial,
For a crowd of ragged, bestial
Beggars at the convent gate?
Would the Vision there remain?
Would the Vision come again?
Then a voice within his breast
Whispered, audible and clear
As if to the outward ear:
"Do thy duty; that is best;
Leave unto thy Lord the rest!"

Straightway to his feet he started,
And with longing look intent
On the Blessed Vision bent,
Slowly from his cell departed,
Slowly on his errand went.

At the gate the poor were waiting,
Looking through the iron grating,
With that terror in the eye
That is only seen in those
Who amid their wants and woes
Hear the sound of doors that close,
And of feet that pass them by ;
Grown familiar with disfavor,
Grown familiar with the savor
Of the bread by which men die !
But to-day, they know not why,
Like the gate of Paradise
Seemed the convent gate to rise,
Like a sacrament divine
Seemed to them the bread and wine.
In his heart the Monk was praying,
Thinking of the homeless poor,
What they suffer and endure ;
What we see not, what we see ;
And the inward voice was saying :
"Whatsoever thing thou doest
To the least of mine and lowest,
That thou doest unto me !"

Unto me ! but had the Vision
Come to him in beggar's clothing,
Come a mendicant imploring,
Would he then have knelt adoring,

Or have listened with derision,
And have turned away with loathing?

Thus his conscience put the question
Full of troublesome suggestion,
As at length, with hurried pace,
Towards his cell he turned his face
And beheld the convent bright
With a supernatural light,
Like a luminous cloud expanding
Over floor and wall and ceiling.

But he paused with awe-struck feeling
At the threshold of his door,
For the Vision still was standing
As he left it there before,
When the convent bell appalling,
From its belfry calling, calling,
Summoned him to feed the poor.
Through the long hour intervening
It had waited his return,
And he felt his bosom burn,
Comprehending all the meaning,
When the Blessed Vision said,
"Hadst thou stayed, I must have fled!"

CHARLEMAGNE

OLGER the Dane and Desiderio,
King of the Lombards, on a lofty tower
Stood gazing northward o'er the rolling plains,
League after league of harvests, to the foot
Of the snow-crested Alps, and saw approach
A mighty army, thronging all the roads
That led into the city. And the King
Said unto Olger, who had passed his youth
As hostage at the court of France, and knew
The Emperor's form and face: "Is Charlemagne
Among that host?" And Olger answered: "No."

And still the innumerable multitude
Flowed onward and increased, until the King
Cried in amazement: "Surely Charlemagne
Is coming in the midst of all these knights!"
And Olger answered slowly: "No; not yet;
He will not come so soon." Then much disturbed
King Desiderio asked, "What shall we do,
If he approach with a still greater army?"
And Olger answered: "When he shall appear,
You will behold what manner of man he is;
But what will then befall us I know not."

Then came the guard that never knew repose,
The Paladins of France; and at the sight
The Lombard King o'ercome with terror cried:
"This must be Charlemagne!" and as before
Did Olger answer: "No; not yet, not yet."

And then appeared in panoply complete
The Bishops and the Abbots and the Priests
Of the imperial chapel, and the Counts;
And Desiderio could no more endure
The light of day, nor yet encounter death,
But sobbed aloud and said: "Let us go down
And hide us in the bosom of the earth,
Far from the sight and anger of a foe
So terrible as this!" And Olger said:
"When you behold the harvests in the fields
Shaking with fear, the Po and the Ticino
Lashing the city walls with iron waves,
Then may you know that Charlemagne is come.
And even as he spake, in the northwest,
Lo! there uprose a black and threatening cloud,
Out of whose bosom flashed the light of arms
Upon the people pent up in the city;
A light more terrible than any darkness,
And Charlemagne appeared; — a Man of Iron!

His helmet was of iron, and his gloves
Of iron, and his breastplate and his greaves
And tassets were of iron, and his shield.

In his left hand he held an iron spear,
In his right hand his sword invincible.
The horse he rode on had the strength of iron,
And color of iron. All who went before him,
Beside him and behind him, his whole host,
Were armed with iron, and their hearts within them
Were stronger than the armor that they wore.
The fields and all the roads were filled with iron,
And points of iron glistened in the sun
And shed a terror through the city streets.

This at a single glance Olger the Dane
Saw from the tower, and turning to the King
Exclaimed in haste: "Behold! this is the man
You looked for with such eagerness!" and then
Fell as one dead at Desiderio's feet.

INDEXES

INDEX OF FIRST LINES

INDEX OF FIRST LINES

328

INDEX OF FIRST LINES

INDEX OF TITLES

INDEX OF TITLES

INDEX OF TITLES

INDEX OF TITLES

CPSIA information can be obtained
at www.ICGtesting.com
Printed in the USA
LVOW13s0237300118
564554LV00024B/135/P